A Life Well Lived

Reflections on Emotional, Intellectual and Spiritual Growth

John Ingram Walker, M.D.

LIFEWORKS PUBLISHING CO.
Fair Oaks, Texas 78015

A Life Well Lived

Lynn Grove Press
Published under the imprint:
LifeWorks Publishing Company
7967 Turf Paradise Lane
Fair Oaks Ranch, TX 78015
210-698-2758 Fax 210-698-9158

Manuscript Preparation: Nanette Burkhardt
Copy Editing: Lynette Weaver
Typesetting: David Nielsen, Historical Publications
Cover Design: Patricia Smithers and Lynn Snyder

Printed and bound in
the United States of America
by Millennia Graphics
Colorado Springs, CO

ISBN 0-9621073-0-1

Fifth printing-July 1999

DEDICATION

To Vicki, whose integrity, refinement and gentle pursuit of excellence are an inspiration to all she meets.

PREFACE

W ith one foot over the threshold of middle age, I find myself more reflective than when the years moved slower and time seemed a stepping stone to success. As I look back on all the people I have seen, the mistakes I've made and the fun I've had in living and practicing medicine, I realize that all of us are in the same boat with the same frustrations and joys, the same struggles and challenges. We all seek meaning and quality in life's opportunities. Here, then, are my thoughts on ways to have excellence in our daily lives. I hope the wide range of topics covered here will inspire the reader to a better life as much as writing these essays has helped me improve my perspective.

ACKNOWLEDGMENTS

I have been blessed with knowing many outstanding people whose love, kind humor, endurance and spunk have inspired me to do better and be better. You will find them in these pages: my grandparents, uncles and aunts, mother, wife and children, my mentors, and my co-workers. To list them all by name would run a risk of leaving out significant others. They know who they are and they will always be dear to me. I especially want to thank Lynette Weaver, who copy-edited this manuscript. She has done a superb job of making certain that every word tells. I also want to thank Robert Krueger, a modern-day Renaissance man who has helped me in many subtle ways. Special praise goes to Mary Powell who, though joining me after the book was written, has been instrumental in the production and distribution of this volume. Finally, I want to thank you, the reader, for reflecting with me. I think you will find that we are friends and that we are bound together by the invisible force that poets call love.

John I. Walker, M.D.
June 1988

CONTENTS

Our Prosperous Thoughts...

Our Prosperous Thoughts

�֍

Yesterday I received a telephone call from my aunt. The telephone line crackled with her enthusiasm and good cheer; the laughter in her voice made the rest of the day sparkle.

It's true that my aunt has been blessed with material wealth, but that's not what makes her happy. She has also had her tragedies and troubles. Her happiness comes not only from externals but from the internal conviction that she is going to enjoy each day to the fullest. She practices what others preach.

The Roman Emperor, Marcus Aurelius, said, "Our life is what our thoughts make it." Emerson summarized what determines our destiny, "A man is what he thinks about all day long." Lincoln said, "Most folks are about as happy as they make up their mind to be." My aunt determined long ago to be happy.

It's strange how certain events trigger fond memories. I vividly remember hearing a guest speaker at Duke University Medical Center in the fall of 1975. The speaker started his academic presentation by thanking the people at Duke for inviting him. He then said, "Being on this campus makes it wonderful to be alive. I enjoyed eating the ham, eggs and toast that

I had for breakfast this morning. The simple things—a good breakfast, enjoying what we have been given, finding pleasure in each day's events—make me happy."

I remember that comment so clearly because the gentleman meant what he was saying. I could tell by the radiant glow in his eyes that he found joy in the simple pleasures of life—eating breakfast, walking on the campus. He enjoyed the ordinary. Whenever I have a particularly enjoyable breakfast, I always remember that man's comments and determine to pay more attention to the little pleasures of life.

I have also noticed that the happiest people serve others. Alfred Adler in his splendid book, *What Life Should Mean to You*, formulates the cure for depression. He says to overcome melancholia, "Try to think every day how you can please someone." Those who are uninterested in other people have the greatest difficulties in life.

If you want to be happy, think happy thoughts. What you think, you are. It's that simple. Every morning, you have a choice: to be happy or to be miserable. Why choose misery?

Around the turn of the century Sibyl F. Partridge wrote a daily program that she entitled, "Just For Today." Here's an edited version of her suggestions for happiness:

1. Just for today I will be happy.
2. Just for today I will try to adjust myself to what is, and not try to change anyone or anything. I will take

my family, my business, and my luck as they come.

4. Just for today I will improve my mind by learning something useful. I will read something that requires effort, thought and concentration.

5. Just for today I will do a good deed for someone.

6. Just for today I will be agreeable. I will dress becomingly, act courteously and be liberal with praise.

7. Just for today I will write down my goals and plans. I will eliminate hurry and indecision.

8. Just for today I will have a quiet half hour all by myself to relax and think of God.

9. Just for today I will be unafraid to enjoy what is beautiful. I will love and believe that those I love, love me.

10. Just for today I will live just this day, today.

That's worth cutting out and pasting on the refrigerator. Read that every day—and practice what you read and you will be happy. Guaranteed.

The poet Milton said, "The mind is its own place, and in itself can make a heaven of hell, a hell of heaven." Dale Carnegie in his book, *How To Stop Worrying And Start Living*, uses quotations of two famous people to underscore Milton's point. Napoleon, who had power, riches and glory said, "I have never known six happy days in my life." Helen Keller, deaf, dumb, and blind, declared, "I have found life so beautiful."

Events, acquisitions and other people cannot give you happiness. Your thoughts alone determine your happiness. Choose happiness.

Wherever You Are, Be There

✄

One evening not long ago I was reading and relaxing in my study, when my daughter cheerfully entered the room and enthusiastically announced, "Dad, we talked about Emerson in English today." Engrossed in my copy of *Sports Illustrated*, I replied, "Hummm, that's interesting," and continued reading.

A few seconds later, the young woman who had been so eager to talk about Emerson tearfully stormed out of the room crying, "You hardly ever listen to me. Maybe that's why I don't talk to you more."

Stunned and shaken I realized that a wonderful opportunity to have a warm interchange of ideas with my daughter was lost and gone forever. Sadly, I remembered an admonishment made by E. James Rohn, "Wherever you are, be there."

Leo Buscaglia, in his book *Love*, reminds us of Thornton Wilder's play *Our Town*. In the poignant third act Emily dies but is allowed by God to return to life for one day. She chooses to relive her twelfth birthday. In one scene she comes down the stairs, pretty in her birthday dress, curls bouncing brightly.

Busy baking a cake for Emily, her mother doesn't notice her. Emily's father is so busy with his papers and concerns about business matters that he walks right by without paying attention to her. Her brother, obsessed with thoughts of his girlfriend, greets her vacantly. Finally, Emily, alone in the center of the stage, says, "I can't, I can't go on. Oh! Oh! It goes so fast. We don't have time to look at one another". She asks, "Do any human beings ever realize life while they live it—every, every minute? . . . That's all human beings are! Just blind people." She then asks God to return her to the comforting grave.

Mothers—bake fewer cakes and pay more attention. Fathers—make less money and more conversation. Our memories depend on how well we listen. As playwright Arthur Miller indicates, "Attention must be paid."

Here are some tips on how to give full attention to the present moment:

DON'T RUMINATE ON THE PAST. Satchel Paige said, "Don't look back, something might be gaining on you." Time spent in looking back deprives us of the opportunity each new day offers for prosperity, growth, and expansion. Learn from the past, then press forward.

AVOID TEDIOUS, BORING CONVERSATION. Time is too short to be bored. If people around you bore you, find more interesting friends and associates. Talk about ideas and events, not other people. Benjamin Franklin's admonition on idle talk is well worth cultivating:

"Speak not but what may benefit others or yourself; avoid trifling conversations."

PAY ATTENTION TO BODY LANGUAGE. Arms folded usually means the person disagrees with you. Hands behind the back usually indicates suspiciousness or withholding. A faraway look indicates boredom. Leaning forward and an open stance or posture indicates interest.

PAY ATTENTION TO ATTITUDES AND FEELINGS AS WELL AS WORDS. Be emotionally involved. Listen to what the person is not saying, as well as what is being said.

CHECK OUT WHAT THE PERSON HAS SAID BY REFLECTING IN YOUR OWN WORDS A SUMMARY OF HIS STATEMENTS. This technique is vitally important when a person is telling you to do something. Be certain that you hear the exact instructions.

AVOID GIVING ADVICE. An East Texas Proverb states, "Don't try to teach a pig to sing; it will irritate the pig and frustrate you."

My daughter and I made up. I thanked her for reminding me about attention and she thanked me for caring enough to change. The experience made me keenly aware of Emerson's words, "The only gift is a portion of thyself." We can all give more of ourselves if we follow that simple rule, "Wherever you are, be there."

Pigeons and Paperboys

⌘

Two friends told me about their recent encounter on the River Walk in San Antonio. They wanted to see the Christmas lights along the river but the crowd that had come to view the splendid decorations made a peaceful stroll difficult. The couple was trying to decide if the beautiful lights merited the struggle with the crowd when a pigeon deposited a message on the man's shoulder. They decided they had seen enough and left.

As they whimsically told their story, I vividly remembered one bright, sunshiny day over two decades ago when, on the verge of flunking out of medical school, I left the administrative building of the University of Texas Medical Branch in Galveston. Worrying about my miserable grades, I was morosely trying to decide what to do with my unhappy life. Suddenly, I felt and heard a plop on my head. When I touched the area I realized that a pigeon had added inspiration to my gloom. After the initial shock, I furtively looked around to see if anyone else had noticed the pigeon's comment on my situation. Then as the absurdity of the situation sunk in, I began to laugh uncontrollably.

The pigeon's intervention became a turning point. Acknowledging that my spirits had sunk to the bottom, I had no choice but to work harder. I stopped worrying and started studying. The improved attitude turned my career and life around. If that pigeon had not been so helpful—who knows?

A similar event occurred three years ago. I had burned myself out at Duke University Medical Center. Feeling unchallenged and unappreciated, I was bored, stagnant, frustrated and depressed. One morning I dragged myself out of bed to go jogging. The misty, cold day reinforced my gloomy spirits. As I plodded along, barely putting one foot in front of the other, the man delivering the early morning paper hit me full in the chest with the Sunday edition.

There was no reason to toss a paper in that particular place in the road; there were no houses around, but for some unexplained reason this stranger tossed a paper that struck me, hard. I was stunned. When I realized that I had been hit by a newspaper, I turned to chase the paperboy, but he was too far away to catch so I jogged on, feeling low and miserable.

It was then that I decided I was overdue for a change. That errantly-tossed paper made me understand that I must do something different with my life. Once again, being a target had shocked me into re-evaluating my attitude. I realized that cultivating my own misery was getting me nowhere. I began looking for new opportunities. A few months later we returned to Texas.

Sometimes we have to be hit hard, literally, to make any changes. It's much easier to continue to make the same mistakes, to plod along using the same inefficient methods, to stay in the old familiar rut; but, to be happy, we must take risks and look for new opportunities, fresh ideas and different behavior patterns.

To stimulate change, here are some questions to ask yourself:

- What have you done in the past that you wish you could change?
- What personality and character traits would you like to improve?
- What three qualities would you like most to see associated with your reputation?
- What personal accomplishments give you the most pride? Are you doing these things often enough?
- Are you putting your time into activities that are important to you?

Life is too short to be miserable. It's time now to make those changes that will allow you to fulfill your potential. If you don't like your job, start looking for something that will stimulate you to grow.

As we eagerly welcome new experiences into our lives, let's accept change with open minds and be receptive to new ideas. Let's work on building personality and character. Let's take time to love, to touch, and to listen. Affirming harmony in God's universe allows us to seek peace and prosperity.

All of us have more opportunity than we can properly develop in a lifetime. The key is finding the opportunity. Start looking. Don't wait for the pigeons and the paperboys to inspire you to new attitudes. Do something different. Do it now.

The Clean-Up Chairman Fights Depression

Recently, I was appointed to the clean-up committee for the high school graduation party because, as the PTA president said, "Dr. Walker is always so positive. He will be able to find something beneficial from cleaning up a mess made by 360 kids, their dates and parents." When I heard that I had been made chairman of the clean-up committee because of my exuberant optimism, I immediately dived into a deep depression.

I'm not always positive. My best friends will tell you I have frailties and character flaws just like everyone else. When I get depressed and frustrated and angry, however, I generally defeat despair using a combination of techniques.

PRAYER. Starting the day with scriptural study and prayer diminishes self-absorption and encourages a balanced perspective. I ask God to forgive my sins; give thanks for His grace and gifts; and ask Him for love, wisdom, peace of mind, joy and faith.

USE COSMIC HUMOR. Whenever I make a mistake, and I make plenty, I try to use humor to put the situation in better perspective. I try not to take myself or my problems too seriously. I write about my mistakes;

therefore, I never run out of material.

STAY ACTIVE. Lincoln said, "I must lose myself in action, lest I wither in despair." Activity is the antidote for depression. We need to remember Winston Churchill's axiom: "Most of the world's work is done by people who do not feel very well." Work cures misery.

READ. Inspirational or humorous literature helps get our minds off our inadequacies and deficiencies. Mysteries and romances help us forget our troubles. Reading biographies about people who overcame adversity gives us encouragement to persist.

CONFRONT PROBLEMS. When a conflict occurs, we do well to deal with the difficulty immediately. Avoiding a problem only increases frustration.

LISTEN TO GOOD MUSIC. Physicians of antiquity used music to regulate the heart rate. From the Renaissance through the 19th century, music was used to treat melancholy. Classical music produces neurophysiologic changes in the parts of the brain which control thinking, emotions, heartbeat, respiration, and muscle tension. Currently, major medical centers use music therapy with patients undergoing spinal surgery and to speed the rate of healing in severe burn cases.

CULTIVATE FRIENDSHIPS. People who have intimate friends are healthier and manage stress better. Sharing feelings with a friend will allow us to ventilate our frustrations and help us develop a better perspective on our problems. Good friends—those who know our faults but like us anyway—can give us suggestions on how to overcome our difficulties.

Healthful, enriching, supportive experience with others is our best defense against self-absorption. If we are feeling deprived of affection, we need to turn our attention to other people. Get in contact, pay attention, listen, and be aware. We become more attractive to others when we pay attention to them and that leads to more affection directed toward us.

EXERCISE. Because stress on one system helps relax the other system, exercise does wonders for emotional stress. The exhaustion that most of us experience is caused by mental fatigue, not physical fatigue. Vigorous physical exercise tones the cardiovascular system, improves joint and muscle flexibility, and increases brain neurochemicals that enhance the feeling of well-being.

CHOOSE HAPPINESS. We cannot change other people or activating events, but we can change our belief about other people and events and consequently have better feelings. The primary factor that determines the quality of our days is our attitude.

ORGANIZATION. Being well-organized and knowing how to set priorities prevents getting frustrated about insignificant issues.

Well, I've listened to music, read a book, cycled ten miles, talked to friends, and laughed at my plight but I'm still upset about being chairman of the clean-up committee. If this essay inspired you to work out your misery, please give me a call. I have a job for you.

Life's Celebrations

⌘

On a recent drive to a San Antonio party, I told my companions about Jim Rohn's statement of love. On an audiocassette program Rohn mentioned that he had taken his wife shopping in Carmel, California. Immediately upon arriving in Carmel, they visited a florist where Mr. Rohn asked for a rose for "my lady." He presented the rose to his wife with a flourish suggesting she carry it around with her as she shopped that day. My friends thought that a rather quaint story and wondered what it would be like to carry a rose while shopping.

On our trip home from the party, the driver of the car noticed a young woman standing on a street corner selling roses. He slammed on his brakes, jumped out of the car, dashed across the street, and purchased two roses, one for "his lady" and one for "my lady." We then went to a restaurant for a midnight breakfast. We asked for two glasses of water for the roses. As we put the roses in the glasses, we had a nice chat with the waitress whose day had been less than bright before meeting us. We laughed and joked and had a good time.

We will remember that midnight breakfast and the

roses long after we have forgotten the party and other events of the day, for we were celebrating life with enthusiasm and spontaneity.

The rose adventure made me reflect on a nice note I received from a regular reader of my column. She said my writing helped her celebrate life. That's nice. We all need to be aware of ways to enjoy life more fully.

My wife and I are fortunate to be blessed with friends who are unpretentious and enjoy doing something a little odd now and then. Of course, I have an excuse for acting odd because I am a psychiatrist. Our friends act odd because they enjoy life. People who are spontaneous and enthusiastic promote goodwill and joy. Fun, joy, and happiness spread just as worry and tension spread. Cultivate friends who spread joy.

This week I got my hair cut. The hairdresser did a marvelous job. She trimmed my hair exactly the way I requested. She clipped around my ears and shaved the back of my neck. She rubbed in some oil to make the hair shine and she dusted off my neck and forehead. She helped me out of the chair with a flourish of the cape. I gave her a compulsory tip and hurried out the door. I didn't tell her what a great job she had done. She was a professional barber; I was an ungrateful customer.

If I had paid as much attention to her as she did to me, I could have made her day. By praising her good work and giving her a warm smile of encouragement, I could have inspired her to continue to do good for others.

A friend told of having his shoes shined in Chicago. The shoeshine man gave him an old fashioned shine. He shined and spit. He polished and buffed. All the time the shineman was talking, whistling and entertaining with his pleasant personality. The shine cost $3 and my friend tipped him $2. He said that the $5 was the best investment that he made all day. Not only did his shoes shine like a mirror, but he felt good about giving a generous tip. He felt and acted like a millionaire and with this millionaire attitude he landed a sizeable sales contract that afternoon.

Be generous with praise. Be generous with money. Reward a good day's work with a fair day's pay. Tithe to your church. Support charities. "Each one must do as he has made up his mind, not reluctantly or under compulsion, for God loves a cheerful giver." (II Cor. 9:7)

The wonderful bonus of cheerful giving is that your generosity always returns to you. "He who sows sparingly will also reap sparingly and he who sows bountifully will also reap bountifully." (II Cor. 9:6)

At a recent dinner party our gracious hostess served us an evening of elegance. She offered her impeccably dressed guests champagne cocktails and dinner by candlelight. We then retired to the living room for baroque music and conversation. That evening of refinement pulled all of us to a higher plane. Instead of talking about people and events, we talked of ideas and purpose.

In seeking a life of refinement we become more civilized. Save up your chip-and-dip money and serve raspberries and cream. Celebrate the fine.

A *Calm and Happy Nature*

⌘

This week I lost my temper. I won't go into details, but I felt as if I were forced to do something against my will. The other party was incessantly persistent and kept interfering with my time schedule. Finally, after several days of conflict, I blew up. I filled the telephone line with vitriolic tirades. I fumed and sputtered. I shouted and turned red. I slammed the receiver down and angrily stalked the floor. It was not a pretty picture.

My actions were inappropriate. Although my rights were infringed upon by the other person, my anger did not help solve the conflict. Learning to control anger distinguishes a civilized person. Channelling anger into productive problem-solving or conflict resolution is appropriate; an unproductive, angry outburst is always uncivilized. Refinement begins with containing anger and controlling the tongue.

Twenty-four hours later I reflected on this angry outburst, trying to understand its source and resolutions. Perhaps these ideas will help all of us deal more appropriately with frustration.

KEEP PRIORITIES IN ORDER. Recently I have been exceedingly busy, trying to cram more and more activities into twenty-four hours. This week my prayers had become brief and repetitive. I had not taken the time to sit for a few minutes, relax, and meditate on the awesome power of God. I had neglected my reading. I had spent too little time with my family, and absolutely no time in just thinking. Writing is one of my top priorities, but I had made no time for it. When I overload my schedule, usually the events that get neglected are the most important ones.

GET THE FACTS. When a conflict arises, make certain that all the facts are understood. Try to distinguish facts from emotion. Never use an intermediary; go directly to the source and negotiate with your antagonist. My anger, in part, occurred because I had not talked directly to my antagonist and I did not have all the facts.

REASON IS BETTER THAN REACTION. When faced with a conflict, try to put yourself in the other person's shoes. Be empathetic. What is he trying to gain? How can you help him get what he wants while at the same time getting your needs met? Can there be a compromise? If your antagonist will not reason with you, get a third party to act as intermediary to help resolve the conflict.

USE YOUR HEAD, NOT YOUR TONGUE. When faced with an irritating situation, ask yourself these important questions: "Will my anger help resolve the issue?" "Will my angry outburst help me achieve my goals?" "Will my anger help me avoid conflicts with others?" "Are these the emotions I want to feel?" When you analyze your angry outbursts in this way, you can easily see that anger does not help protect your life or health.

SUBSTITUTE HUMOR FOR ANGER. Try to view the conflict in a humorous way. You can say things to yourself that will help relieve tension, "Well, the turkeys are gobbling me up again." Try to view the conflict as another example of the absurdity of life by separating yourself from the emotion and looking at the struggle with a detached third eye. You can say to yourself, "Isn't it foolish to see two human beings struggling against each other in this senseless way?" Laugh at yourself and don't take yourself so seriously. Remember that life is short. Energy spent on anger can be put to better use.

ANTICIPATE. Remember that, "This too will pass." No matter how difficult the struggle may seem, the conflict will eventually pass and what you are angry about today will be insignificant a week from now.

Although I have settled down a little now, the telephone lines are still smoking. I have probably made a life-long enemy. At least two to three other people consider me a fool. But I've learned something from the encounter and resolve, with God's help, to do better next time.

Resolving to Appreciate

⌘

This past week my wife and I took a trip to New York. I was not fun to travel with—I griped and complained almost all the way. The flight was late; the cabin was cramped; the service was poor. When we arrived in New York, the cab driver would not open the trunk and wanted me to put my bags in the front seat. I called him lazy; he called me inconsiderate, using an indirect vocabulary that clearly got the point across.

Finally, as my wife and I were getting ready for bed and I was complaining vociferously about the hotel prices in New York, we both broke into spontaneous laughter. We talked about how ridiculously petty I had been, and I remembered what humorist Charlie Jarvis said, "We get on an airline that takes us a thousand miles and complain if we are five minutes late." I resolved, then and there, never to complain about insignificant issues. Here is how I am going to keep my resolution:

APPRECIATE LIFE'S BLESSINGS. My wife and I were flying to New York City to celebrate her birthday. It was long after college before I ever flew in an airplane. Over two decades later, I had become so cynical and travel-worn that I was complaining about the privilege of being able to go to New York City and attend a play. Twenty years ago I would have been bug-eyed with excitement. I could recapture that excitement by paying attention to the privilege, not the price.

On our return flight I sat next to a New York City stock room clerk who had been on twenty-four flights in the last year. He happily talked about the places he had been and the wonderful people he had met. When breakfast was served, he ate with gusto and, after finishing, exclaimed, "Boy, was that good!" He was a simple man but he enjoyed life much more than the pinstriped executives who filled the plane.

PAY ATTENTION TO WHAT IS IMPORTANT. It is important to let my wife know that she is special to me, that I love her kind, gentle ways, and that I appreciate her support and encouragement, her sacrifice, and her compromises. I want her to remember my emotional strength, sincerity, and integrity. I don't want to be thought of as a griper and complainer. I don't want to be remembered as a sorehead or a cynic. Developing spiritually, emotionally and intellectually, and helping those around us grow is important. Minor inconveniences are unimportant.

CULTIVATE HUMOR. George Vaillant, M.D., in his studies of Harvard graduates, has shown the use of humor to be an extremely effective method for achieving success. Vaillant has studied Harvard graduates over a lifetime. He found that successful graduates had five traits that he calls mature defense mechanisms.

These mature defense mechanisms are altruism, suppression, anticipation, sublimation, and humor. Altruism is the unselfish giving of time and efforts to others; suppression is the conscious failure to think about negative issues; anticipation is goal-directed planning for the future; sublimation is channeling aggressive drives into productive work; and humor is responding to the stress of life with good cheer, wit, and perspective. Laughter helps heal hurt.

I would have been much better company on the trip if I had started laughing with the first little foul-up. For example, when we found ourselves squashed in the cramped airplane, I could have said, "I've always wanted to experience flying as a canned sardine," or "With everyone bringing their luggage on board, I bet we could get a great seat in the baggage compartment." These aren't show-stopping lines, but they would have brightened the mood and lightened the tension. To the cab driver I could have said, "This is the first time my bags have made it to New York City. I'm so happy to have them with me, I'll be glad to put them anywhere you want." Again, not really funny, but showing good cheer.

After our laugh in the hotel room that night, the following day was one of the best of our lives. We both enjoyed what we had been given. We laughed and talked, held hands, and showed appreciation for each other. And I didn't complain, not even when two breakfast rolls, orange juice, and coffee cost $32.58.

Happiness Is A Ten (Make That Eleven)

⌘

A wonderful book came across my desk today, called Emotional Health. One in a series entitled *The Prevention Total Health System*, this book contains hundreds of useful tips on ways to have a healthier emotional outlook. Although no one has a single formula for happiness, most mental health professionals agree on the factors that contribute to happiness. Here, according to the experts at *Prevention Magazine*, are ten ways to be happier:

1. APPRECIATE OUR UNIQUE ABILITIES. Only when we love ourselves can we give unconditional love to others. According to Perry W. Buffington, an Atlanta psychologist, we can begin to appreciate ourselves by avoiding self-criticism. We would do well to monitor what we're thinking, to consider if we are really as bad as we tell ourselves we are. Then, instead of negative self-talk, we can begin to forgive ourselves and develop our talents.
2. SEEK THE LOVING LIFE. Love answers many problems. Love means forgiving others; love means understanding, but not judging others; love means helping others develop their potential. When we focus attention on someone else, we

begin to feel better about ourselves.

3. JOIN THE WORKADAY WORLD. Almost everyone becomes miserable when there is nothing to do for prolonged periods of time. Because activity cures misery, we must become involved with life by motivating ourselves to stay busy. Life is a banquet—feast on it.

4. ENJOY THE POWER OF TOUCH. When we touch others we confirm that we are a part of—not apart from—humanity. James Hardison, Ph.D., a San Diego psychologist and the author of *Let's Touch* says, "It is through touching that we are able to fulfill a large share of our human needs and, in doing so, to attain happiness. By touching someone we can affirm our friendship, communicate important messages, promote health and bring about love." We must not be reluctant to display goodwill through pats on the back, warm handshakes, cordial hugs.

5. LIVE ONE DAY AT A TIME. Worrying about the past or fretting about the future will always ruin a perfectly good day. Worry is negative goal setting; regret is negative memory programming. While worry ties up energy that could be used for productive problem solving and regret wastes time that could be used for building good memories, living one day at a time guarantees an enriching life. We can focus on doing our best one day at a time. One good day for seven days makes one good week; one good week for fifty-two weeks

makes one good year; one good year for seventy-five years makes a good lifetime.

6. FILL THE DAYS WITH LAUGHTER. He who laughs, lasts. Looking at our failings in a humorous way allows us to be more flexible and take in stride what life dishes out.

7. EXERCISE REGULARLY. Stress on the physical system helps relax the mental system. Exercise tones the cardiovascular system and at the same time elevates self-confidence, diminishes anxiety, cancels depression and provides a natural euphoria.

8. SEARCH FOR MEANING. Each person must have a purpose in life that makes the striving worthwhile. We can find purpose through study, prayer, and self-knowledge. Zest comes from doing things we care deeply about.

9. CULTIVATE VARIETY. Each individual can endeavor to lead a balanced life—giving a fair day's work for a fair day's pay and being active in community and social affairs. To stimulate creativity learn to play a musical instrument, paint, attend a drama class. Maintain a hobby, plant a garden, become a pet owner. Play and have fun like a child.

10. GIVE TO OTHERS. Life is like an echo—we get back what we send out. If we send out love we receive love in return. To expand our caring relationships, we can devote ourselves to an altruistic organization, one whose purpose will establish social bonds and result in positive feedback from others.

Interestingly, these mental health experts left out one of the most important aspects of emotional well-being—spiritual growth. When we feed the soul, we find deeper levels of happiness.

Going With The Flow

⌘

At a state high school basketball playoff game, I noticed that the two teams had contrasting approaches. One team played the game with relaxed enthusiasm; the players exuded joy and confidence. During time-outs the coach spent time diagramming plays and reinforcing the enthusiastic attitude. The other team played with desperate intensity; its members were mechanical and fearful. Their coach spent time-outs yelling and screaming at the team, telling them what they did wrong. Both teams were equally talented. Guess who won?

All athletes know that relaxed confidence allows better play. The relaxed, euphoric state when things seem to go just right, when we feel alive and fully attentive to what we are doing, is known as flow or peak performance. Flow, a trance-like state, is characterized by total absorption in the task, focused concentration, distortion, and altered sensory perception.

John Brodie, the former NFL quarterback, said that when he was playing at peak performance, rushing defensive linemen seemed to come at him in slow motion. Michael Jordan reports that when he scored sixty-three points against the Boston Celtics in an NBA Playoff Game, he was so absorbed in his play that he was totally unaware of the score or the game clock. Tennis players, when they are playing at their peak, are described as being "in a tree."

Without doubt we perform better when we are totally absorbed in the task. We do better in athletics, in business, and in our relationships with others when we are in a state of relaxed concentration. How can we cultivate this state of peak performance called flow? Here are some ideas.

When we are trying to do well in any task, we can concentrate on relaxing by saying to ourselves, "Relax and let go." Even daily, routine tasks can cause us to become tense and irritable. Headaches, backaches, stomachaches, and muscle pains generally indicate too much tension. When we become more aware of our body tension, we can relieve it by telling ourselves to relax.

If we have faith in God who loves us and cares for us, all things are possible. "I can do all things through Him who strengthens me" (Philippians 4:13). Indeed, with total faith we would always perform at our peak at all times. Through scriptural study and prayer, we can learn to turn our lives over to God. Faith is more than saying we believe, it also means that we act our belief, i.e., we let go and let God.

Performing at peak levels requires concentration, composure, and confidence. To acquire these skills demands practice. All athletes practice the mechanics of their sport repetitively to compete skillfully; successful business people read, study, and attend educational meetings to enhance their business skills.

We need also to practice successful living techniques for cultivating wisdom and harmony in daily tasks. When faced with a stressful conflict, we essentially have three choices: 1) fight it; 2) flee from it; 3) flow. To learn to flow when things get tense around the house, practice composure and a calm attitude. The more we think calmness and relaxation, the easier it becomes to deal with conflict and tension.

All peak performers visualize success. Before shooting a free throw, skilled basketball players see the ball ripping through the net. Before the great golfer, Jack Nicklaus, hits each ball, he vividly pictures where he wants the ball to go. Likewise, if we visualize a happy home, we will work toward a happy home. If we visualize business success, our positive expectations will enhance peak performance.

Our individual stresses diminish when we take a cosmic view of life—when we consider the vastness of the universe, our daily irritants become insignificant. Most of what we worry about never happens and unproductive thinking ties up our energy and prevents us from performing at our peak. Who can remember last year's concerns? A year from now who will remember today's worries? A cosmic view of life encourages concentration on goals instead of worries.

On a recent ski trip I heard a fellow vacationer exclaim, as she awkwardly struggled up an icy embankment toward the ski lift, "Are we having fun yet?" This question caused the rest of us awkwardly struggling individuals to laugh at ourselves. It made me think we would do well to ask ourselves each day, "Am I having fun?" If we are not having fun, why not?

Life is meant to be enjoyed. If we are going through life tense, uptight, worried, and anxious, we miss the fun of life's challenge and we diminish our chance of success. We cannot perform at our best without enjoyment. Laughter and joy ensure a relaxed euphoria that enhances peak performance.

Wisdom and Change For A Dime

�֎

On a recent speaking engagement to Carlsbad, New Mexico, I determined to take a side trip to visit Mary Louise Lynch, publisher of the *Hudspeth County Herald* in Dell City, Texas, and a lady with whom I had become acquainted through correspondence. Because Dell City was a short trip over the Guadalupe Mountains and the day was aglow with sunshine, I decided to charter a plane. Unfortunately, my imagination was richer than reality and every attempt to arrange a charter failed.

Jeanne and Kathy, the two motel desk clerks who had been trying to help, were giving up hope, but I bet each a nickel that I could somehow catch a flight, and set out for the airport. I found the staff at the airport's charter service no more helpful in person than they had been over the phone and their discouraging, negative nods became more vigorous with each approach I tried. Obviously, these people weren't as enthusiastic about my trip as I was.

Just as I was about to change my dime for two nickels I noticed a man walking toward the terminal. Informed that he had just landed, I asked him if he would take me to Dell City. I discovered later that he and three friends had flown commercially from Germany to Austin, where they had leased two Piper Archers and were on a two-week flying tour of the Western United States. With a little gentle persuasion, two of the Germans decided that a side trip to Dell City would make an interesting excursion. Within five minutes we were off.

The landscape was brilliant with sunshine, giving an emancipated sense of freedom from all cares and responsibilities as we flew higher and higher to get safely over the Guadalupe Mountains. Once across, we entered a modern-day Shangri-la. In contrast to the desert in New Mexico, Dell Valley's irrigated farm land was lush with vegetation—alfalfa, cotton and fruit grow abundantly there.

Dell City has only 625 people, but the size of the town did not make the unmarked airstrip easier to find and we circled the village a couple of times before landing. Just as we touched down, Mary Louise Lynch, having heard us circling, drove up.

I instantaneously became a fan of Mary Louise who, with quiet enthusiasm, drove me around the town (it didn't take long). She then showed me her pressroom and a May 1988 *Smithsonian* article comparing the *Hudspeth County Herald* with William Allen White's legendary Emporia, Kansas, *Gazette*. Then she took me next door to meet Mary Moseley.

Mrs. Moseley told me that she had survived two cancer surgeries through faith, prayer, and a positive attitude. She had learned to live, she said, by using the dynamic laws of healing: "...to forgive; let go of anger; let go of the past; and cultivate loving relationships." Avoiding "what if's" helped her live each day to the fullest. "Find something to smile about—find it now!" she said. I could have flown from San Antonio to Chicago for a decade and not heard a better inspirational message.

After thanking Mary Moseley for her message of good cheer, I hopped in Mary Louise's Cadillac and she whisked me back to the airstrip. A good tailwind reduced the return flight to thirty minutes. Soon I was far away from the experiences of Dell City, Texas, but memories of my adventure still bring feelings of exhilaration and emancipation.

Once we touched down I couldn't wait to get back to the motel lobby. Arriving there, I presented Jeanne and Kathy a card signed by Mary Louise Lynch certifying that I had made it to Dell City (by airplane). We all had a good laugh together as the clerks cheerfully handed me their nickels.

Carried away by my own grandiloquence, I used the opportunity to make a speech. It was a good speech, but melodramatic, one that would have made William Jennings Bryan proud. I said, "I want you to take these nickels and paste them on your desk where you can see them every day and when life gets extra tough and you don't think you have the courage to go on, I want you to look at those nickels and remember: never, never, never give up. If you want something badly enough, you can get it."

I could tell by the looks from Jeanne and Kathy that they liked my speech and it made me happy to have met them and Mary Moseley and Mary Louise Lynch and my German pilots and to have flown to Dell City. It was a wonderful morning, one of those rare times that I will remember forever.

As I signed my bill, checked out of the motel and walked out the door, I realized that when times get hard Jeanne and Kathy will remember my speech, look at those nickels pasted on the desk—and spend them!

Day By Day, Better And Better

❇

Emile Coue, the French chemist and pioneer of auto-suggestion, coined the phrase, "Day by day, in every way, I'm getting better and better."

Those who scoff at Coue's aphorism, misunderstand a powerful concept. Words energize our lives because our minds transform thought into action. Negative words induce poor results; positive words generate beneficial outcomes.

We frequently fill our minds with negative thoughts that gradually undermine our emotional well-being and strength of character. For example, we might say, "That job is a pain in the neck" only to develop a headache several hours later. A tennis player might say, "I always choke on the big points," and it is he who loses the important game. Or someone might say, "My reports are always late" and he's right.

Studies have shown that by changing our words, we can change our behavior. Therefore, it is best to say, "Day by day, in every way, I'm getting better and better" than to say, "Life is a drag and no fun."

Likewise, when imagination and willpower are in conflict, the imagination always wins. Imagination is a powerful tool for success. Force of will never keeps you on a diet, but proper visualization will. Visualization will make you a winner on the golf course or tennis court, and it will enable you to be more successful in business and in your daily life. It will help you break negative habits. Here are some tips on proper visualization and thinking.

To be effective, visualization must occur when the mind is in Alpha rhythm. Electrical energy is produced by the brain and can be measured by an electroencephalograph (EEG). This energy rhythm is measured in cycles per second (CPS). When you are wide awake and working, you are in Beta rhythm (14 CPS); when you are daydreaming, you are in Alpha rhythm (7-14 CPS); when you are in a light sleep, you are in Theta rhythm (4-7 CPS); and when you are in a deep sleep, you are in Delta rhythm (below 4 CPS). Alpha rhythm is the time that your imagination is most powerful.

The easiest way to enter Alpha rhythm is through meditation techniques. Simply get into a relaxed position, gently close your eyes, and repeat to yourself: "Breathe in relaxation and breathe out tension." The constant repetition of saying the same phrase over and over again drives you into Alpha rhythm. Within a few minutes you will find yourself relaxed, comfortable and slightly drowsy—then you are in Alpha rhythm.

After you have entered Alpha rhythm, visualize a solution to a problem that you are having by creating a mental screen as suggested by Jose Silva, founder of the Silva Mind Control Method. In your mind's eye picture a large movie screen that is about six feet in front of you. Now, on your mental screen re-create a recent event which involved a problem. Relive this problem for a minute and then gently push this scene off the screen by replacing it with what you want to occur.

For example, if you are fifty pounds overweight, initially visualize yourself the way you are currently. Then gradually change the image of yourself and see yourself weighing twenty-five pounds less. Concentrate on exactly how you would look and how much better you would feel. Next, replace this visualization with an image of yourself at your ideal body weight, weighing fifty pounds less than you do now. Experience this scene vividly as if it had actually happened. Stay with the visualization for a while to get the full feel of it.

To awaken, count from one to five, suggesting to yourself as you count slowly that you will feel wide awake, alert, and happy when you get to the count of five. This powerful visualization technique will work with any problem and will help you break old habits and turn you into a winner.

Whenever you find yourself worrying about a problem during the day, stop worrying and start visualizing success. Simply take a deep breath in, breathe in relaxation, breathe out tension, and picture a brief visual image of success. This visual image of succeeding will enable you to meet your expectations.

Whenever you find yourself talking negatively, replace negative words with positive words. Shift your attention from the thing you are worried about to the problem's solution. Your mind can occupy itself with only one thought at a time, so give attention to the positive rather than the negative. Cultivate positives: happiness instead of sadness, courage instead of anxiety, power instead of weakness.

Visualize and talk to yourself as if you are already successful and you will find yourself succeeding. Whenever you find yourself thinking negatively, affirm, "Day by day, in every way, I'm getting better and better."

It's What Possesses You

�֍

Recently over lunch, friends and I discussed success. One friend reminded us that speaker and author, Earl Nightingale, defined success as "the persistent pursuit of a worthy goal." I then quoted Shakespeare, "He is well paid who is well satisfied," indicating that success depends on the individual's perception of success.

Because quoting Shakespeare stimulates intellectual conversation, the aphorisms began to pour forth. Another friend quoted Emerson, "If a man can write a better book, preach a better sermon, or make a better mousetrap than his neighbor, though he built his house in the woods, the world will make a beaten path to his door." A fourth friend fired off this quote, "Nothing succeeds so well as success." None of us could name the originator of that hackneyed expression. Later I looked it up. Talleyrand said it first.

The intellectual in the crowd quoted Addison, "If you wish success in life, make perseverance your bosom friend, experience your wise counselor, caution your elder brother, and hope your guardian genius." The conversation quickly deteriorated after that as we began to talk about the stock market, golf scores, and other depressing things.

The discussion, however, later inspired me to do further research on success. I relistened to the audiocassette tape, *The Psychology of Achievement,* by Brian Tracy. On that tape Tracy gives six requirements for success:

1. Peace of mind—freedom from guilt, fear, and anger.
2. Good health and a high level of energy—life is unsatisfactory without health or energy.
3. Loving relationships—intimate, mature relationships with others.
4. Financial freedom—it's difficult to enjoy life when we are worried over lack of money.
5. Commitments to worthy ideals and goals—these give meaning and purpose in life.
6. Self-actualization—becoming everything we are capable of becoming gives a feeling of personal fulfillment.

Tracy goes on to discuss several basic rules governing success.

The law of cause and effect indicates that we have the ability to influence the outcome of our lives by our actions and thoughts. If we want a good outcome in life, we must think and act appropriately. "For whatever a man sows, that he will also reap." (Galatians 6:7). Life is designed for the planters; many of those in need are needy primarily because they fail to plant anything—they fail to put forth effort.

In almost every gymnasium there reads a sign, "No Pain, No Gain." That axiom is true in any life endeavor. We grow from the pain and the push. We need to set goals and make measurable progress by checking ourselves daily to see if our behavior matches our goals.

Being casual about personal development brings a life of casualness. As speaker E. James Rohn reminds us, many of our problems are caused by doing less than we can, or, as Jim puts it, "Doing less than we can messes up our minds."

The law of belief indicates that whatever we believe—with feeling—becomes our reality. "Therefore I tell you, whatever you ask in prayer, believe that you have received it, and it will be yours" (Mark 11:24). The law of attraction indicates that we attract those people and circumstances that harmonize with our dominant thoughts. We can dramatically improve the quality of our life by taking control of our minds. If we expect good things to happen then they will happen because we attract what we think about.

While success, like beauty, is in the eye of the beholder, to be successful requires that we understand the laws of the universe and that we work at improving our characters and our personalities. As my grandfather said, "It's not what you possess; it's what possesses you that makes life worthwhile."

Dream, Dare, Do

This week I attended the Annual Award Banquet for the Optimist Club. Seeing the multitalented student recipients thank their parents for their continuing support inspired good will and, yes, optimism. These award winners, as all optimists, demonstrated three character traits: they dreamed, they dared, they did.

All great optimists are great dreamers. According to speaker Earl Nightingale, "American people can have anything they want; the trouble is they don't know what they want. Their dreams are not vivid enough."

You are what you dream about all day long. Visualize exactly what you want. Visualize it vividly enough and you will successfully find a way to make your dreams come true.

After attending a seminar led by speaker and author Ed Foreman, a lady decided that she wanted to acquire a Datsun 280-Z. She cut out a picture of a Datsun 280-Z, pasted it on her refrigerator and gazed fondly at the photograph day after day. Finally she realized that to get the Datsun, she would have to find some way of making extra money. After searching for the right opportunity, she decided to go into the Tupperware business. Within six months, she had made enough money to purchase the Datsun, and, more importantly, she had found something to get excited about. She discovered sales and organizational skills that she had previously failed to recognize. She began having fun and spreading good will.

All optimists dare. They take risks and do something. Michael Korda, Editor-in-Chief of Simon and Schuster Publishing Company and author of the best sellers *Power* and *Success*, said there are four characteristics required of successful people: they are unafraid to take risks; they never refuse an opportunity; they don't feel guilty about their ambition; and, they dress for success.

Most successful people have failed many times, but they dare to keep trying; they persist. Thomas J. Watson, the founder of IBM, said that to be successful, you should double your failure rate. The more failures you make, the quicker you learn and the faster you move toward success.

Hank Aaron led the baseball world in home runs; he also struck out more times than any other baseball player. Babe Ruth hit 714 home runs; he struck out 1,330 times. But we don't think about Aaron's or Ruth's strike-outs, we think about their home runs. It's not how many times you strike out that counts; it's how many times you keep swinging that determines whether you are successful or not.

To find meaningful work, focus on ideas that enable you to better serve others. Spend the first few minutes every morning in prayer asking God to give you those qualities that will enable you to succeed—love, wisdom joy, faith, and peace of mind. Each morning ask God to help you accomplish your goals.

Intelligent action begins with an organized plan for learning. Read, listen to audiocassettes, attend seminars and cultivate friends with fresh ideas. Reading for thirty to sixty minutes a day will enable you to read a book a week. According to seminar leader Brian Tracy, reading fifty-two books a year will give you an enormous edge, because most people read less than one book a year. Moreover, 58% of adults never read a non-fiction book from cover to cover after leaving high school.

If you drive 12,000 miles a year, you spend 500 hours a year in your automobile. Tracy translates this travel time into the equivalent of a university semester. Spending 500 hours a year listening to audiocassette programs in your car can provide the critical edge that will propel you toward success.

Be an optimist. Dream big. Dare to pursue your dreams. Do something. Do it now.

The Power Of Positive Thinking Revisited

�֎

Last week our Sunday School class discussed hope. Toward the end of the hour a member who had impressed the class with his bright mind, ready wit, and warm sense of humor commented on Norman Vincent Peale's book, *The Power of Positive Thinking.* He said he had found the book exceedingly useful in times of crisis. He had been helped by Peale's advice that even when life is difficult, the correct attitude can enable us to manage daily stresses better.

The class' comments stimulated me to pull Peale's book off the shelf and read through it once again. As I opened those dusty pages, a wave of nostalgia flooded my spirit. Two times in my life this book enabled me to overcome hardships. When I was about to flunk out of college my freshman year, Peale's wise words gave me courage to work harder. Again, as a first year medical student, I felt overwhelmed by inferior feelings. Convinced that everyone in my class was much brighter, I was consumed by worry. I couldn't concentrate on my studies. Reading Peale between semesters enabled me to stop comparing myself to others and start working.

The Power of Positive Thinking is not Pollyanna optimism

nor is it candy-coated reassurance. Simple, yes; super-ficial, no. To summarize Peale's book does it little justice. For the book to help, a person must read it many times and meditate upon it daily. With those admonishments, here follows a one-paragraph summary:

Failure is caused by wallowing in self-pity and negative self-absorption. We succeed when we turn our lives over to a higher power and when we call upon the invisible positive forces in the universe. There is a God who cares for us and will help us. All we need to do is believe firmly in this higher power. If we call on the universal power and visualize success, we will succeed.

Peale's book is divided into seventeen chapters rang-ing from "Believing in Yourself" to "How to Draw Upon That Higher Power." Every page is filled with inspirational examples and dynamic quotes. No empty words here.

In chapter one, Dr. Karl Menninger, of the Menninger Psychiatric Clinic, is quoted as saying, "Attitudes are more important than facts." This sentence reminded me of a delightful story about attitude told by a friend whose radiant personality reflects his understanding of this crucial subject.

My friend, a highly successful vice-president of sales for a multi-million dollar company, told me how the enthusiasm of a group of young trainees had resulted in numerous sales that cynical sales veterans were una-ble to achieve. These eager, young recruits, too ignorant to know about the effects of the bad economy, were setting records. The veterans, who had superb technical skills but believed business to be bad, were unable to make sales. This businessman said that he preferred young, enthusiastic people with poor technical skills over superb technicians with poor attitudes. He reiterated Karl Menninger's statement, "Attitudes are more important than facts."

Another friend recently told how he used the visualizing techniques suggested by Peale in applying for an executive position. He was one of four semifinalists from an applicant pool of sixty outstanding individuals. Preparing for his final interview, he began to visualize exactly how he would feel working for the company. He vividly pictured himself walking down the hall toward work, how wonderful it would feel to sit in his spacious office, and how excited he would be about his challenging position. He established a clear image of himself already having the job. On his final interview he did exceptionally well—and he was hired.

How did visualizing success enable him to get the job? In the first place, the visualization enabled him to relax and perform confidently during the interview. But more importantly, the visualization, similar to prayer, drew on that higher, universal power that allowed "success unexpected in the common hour."

It's good to have friends who spread warmth and reinforce right thinking. It's nice to be reminded how far we have come and how much we have to learn on our journey Godward. The Sunday School class discussion brought back nostalgic memories of a scared young man bothered by inadequate thoughts and made me realize that positive thinking does make that journey more pleasant.

Thoughts, Perfected By Degrees

❋

Perfectionists and pessimists have miserable lives. They make life intolerable for their families, limit themselves at work, reject goodness and joy, and fill up psychiatrists' offices. They are dysphoric and depression-prone. Perfectionists and pessimists tend to become depressed for several reasons:

* Perfectionists focus on negative events rather than positive.
* Perfectionists make sweeping negative generalizations about themselves, the world, and the future. Holiday depressives might say, for example, "The turkey was overcooked and Christmas was ruined."
* Perfectionists say "ought to" and "must" more than optimists, who are much easier on themselves.
* Perfectionists make impossible demands on themselves. They seek the perfect friends, perfect dinners, perfect in-laws. Unfortunately, we live in an imperfect world; therefore, those seeking perfection are frequently disappointed.
* Pessimists attribute success to luck, whereas optimists attribute success to skill.
* Pessimists blame failures on poor skill; optimists blame failure on bad luck.

* Pessimists remember their failures; optimists recall their successes.

If you are a perfectionist and prone to pessimism, you must work hard to overcome bad habits of thought and mind. Make a valid attempt to accentuate the positive; eliminate negative self-talk and negative mental tapes. Refuse to think or talk negatively. View your past mistakes as an opportunity for growth. There is only one way to develop good judgment—learn from your poor judgment.

Look for the good in situations. Surround yourself with life—a puppy, a plant, an aquarium filled with lively fish. Remind yourself, "A joyful heart does good like medicine; a broken spirit dries the bones" (Proverbs 17:22).

Take stock of where you have been and where you want to go. See and visualize yourself as being successful. Be bold. Act, change, grow. The future is yours to enjoy.

Learn to think more positively by performing the rational ABC's wherein A is the activating event; B is your belief about the event; and C is the consequence of the belief. You cannot change the activating event or other people, but you can change your beliefs about events and others and consequently have good feelings and appropriate behavior. Ask yourself these five questions:
* Is my thinking based on obvious fact?
* Will my thinking help protect my life and health?
* Will my thinking help me achieve my goals?

* Will my thinking help me avoid interpersonal conflicts?
* Will my thinking help me feel the emotions I want to feel?

You have a choice to be happy or to be miserable. Thinking in ways that will protect your life and health, help you achieve your goals, help you avoid interpersonal conflicts, and feel the emotions you want to feel will allow you to enjoy life more.

An article published in *Science* indicated that smiling behavior—turning your lips upward in a smiling-type position—actually increases chemicals in the brain that promote happy feelings. The muscles used in smiling constrict tiny vessels supplying blood to the brain. This minuscule decrease in brain blood flow causes an increase in the neurochemicals that help us feel better emotionally. Forcing yourself to smile, as ludicrous as it may seem, allows you to feel better.

There are many other ways to help yourself feel better:
* Look for the good in yourself and others.
* Be active. It's impossible to be depressed when you're active. Work cures misery.
* Postpone thinking of problems until they come up.
* Take time off when you find yourself becoming overtired.
* Have varied interests—pursue a hobby or recreational activity.
* Cultivate a sense of humor.

Life can be better if we can stop trying to be perfect and accept the frailties of ourselves and others. If we can learn to forgive and forget, we can overcome most problems.

The Prosperity Book

※

As a young newspaper reporter, Napoleon Hill came to the attention of Robert L. Taylor, former Governor of Tennessee who employed Hill to write "success stories" about famous men and assigned him to interview steel multimillionaire, Andrew Carnegie. At the conclusion of the interview Carnegie suggested that Hill organize the world's first philosophy of individual achievement. This suggestion launched Napoleon Hill's distinguished writing career. Hill spent a lifetime of research synthesizing the success ideas of five hundred wealthy men including Henry Ford, Thomas Edison and Andrew Carnegie into the first practical "how to" book, *Think and Grow Rich*, originally published in 1937.

According to W. Clement Stone who amassed a personal fortune of $40 million as founder of Combined Insurance Company of America, *Think and Grow Rich*, has motivated more people to acquire great wealth than any book written in this century. After fifty-one years, it remains one of the top ten best selling business and success books each year.

Hill writes, "Anybody can wish for riches, and most people do, but only a few know that a definite plan plus a burning desire for wealth are the only means of accumulating wealth." Hill's "Thirteen Steps to Riches" provide a working blueprint to wealth for anyone willing to pay the price in time and effort. Here are nine of his recommendations for riches:

DESIRE. Because there are no limitations to the mind except those we acknowledge, Hill gives six ways to turn desires into success:
1. Fix your mind on the exact type of success you desire.
2. Determine exactly what you intend to give in return for your success.
3. Establish a definite date when you intend to be successful.
4. Write out a clear, concise plan to achieve your success.
5. Read the written statement aloud twice daily and as you read, see, feel, and believe yourself already in possession of the success.
6. Begin at once to put this plan into action.

FAITH. Faith is indispensable for success. Faith is induced and strengthened by instructions you give your unconscious mind. The dominating thoughts of the mind will eventually reproduce themselves in outward physical action and gradually transform themselves into physical reality.

AUTOSUGGESTION. Self-suggestion influences the unconscious mind to begin completion of conscious thoughts whether they are positive or negative. We can train ourselves to feed our minds with positive thoughts and expectations. When we gain the ability to control the thoughts that reach the unconscious mind, successful behavior will ultimately follow.

SPECIALIZED KNOWLEDGE. Knowledge paves the road to riches. When knowledge is organized into a definite action plan, a positive outcome is inevitable. Knowledge can be gained through experience, education, personal relationships, people, schooling, reading, listening to educational tapes, and taking special training courses.

IMAGINATION. With imagination the desire is given shape, form, and action. Visualizing success ensures success.

DECISION. While indecision is a major cause of failure, a decisive mind generates tremendous extra power. When a plan is made, act on it.

PERSISTENCE. Having a definite purpose, cultivating a vivid desire, acquiring accurate knowledge, and gaining the cooperation of others will enable one to persist in the determination to be successful. Successful people make a habit of "keeping on keeping on."

THE MASTER MIND. Every successful individual can become more successful by meeting regularly with a small group of people to make plans for continuing success. Hill calls this group the "master mind." Thoughts can carry a "magnetism" which attracts related thoughts, making several minds work as one. When a group functions in harmony, the increased energy created through that alliance generates ideas and enthusiasm.

STIMULI OF THE MIND. In addition to an alliance with a master mind group, the human mind is stimulated by love, music, and friendship. Successful people require a variety of emotional experiences for inspiration and renewal.

While wealth does not guarantee happiness, the principles advocated by Napoleon Hill will enable us to enjoy life more. We feel good when we use all of our creative energy.

Street Smarts

Smart people succeed because they are smart. Smart is not equivalent to intelligent, however. We all know many people with high I.Q.'s who fail. Smart means savvy, as in street smart. Here's how to be successfully smart:

DEVELOP SOCIAL SKILLS. We all know people with superb academic intelligence who lack social intelligence—the ability to listen well and to be sensitive toward others. Those with poor interpersonal skills have difficulty taking criticism. When confronted with a mistake, their egos and emotions get in the way of learning methods for improvement. They deny responsibility, blame others and have difficulty controlling their tempers.

Because social incompetents tend to blame others, co-workers and subordinates take pleasure in helping them fail. One day at an airport I noticed a pin-striped executive yelling at a baggage handler. The more abusive the executive became, the calmer the skycap seemed. After the executive left, I heard the porter say to his associate, "The chief there is going to Chicago, but his bags are going to Dubuque."

Those who seek the cooperation of others, who want

their luggage to arrive at the proper destination, work on mastering social skills. Social intelligence, like good manners, can be learned. To improve social skills:
1. Be empathetic—put yourself in the other person's shoes.
2. Admit your mistakes simply, clearly and quickly.
3. Give others credit for their good work.
4. Make others feel important.
5. Work on being kind, gentle and thoughtful.
6. Be cheerful, enthusiastic, and optimistic.
7. Help other people get what they want.

RIGHT FIT. Successful people fit their abilities, interests, personality style and values with their work. For example, outspoken, risk-oriented individuals would do poorly as accountants; but they may thrive as entrepreneurs. Understanding your core value—what you stand for and your purpose for living—can enable you to choose the right occupation. Here's how to find out if you are on the correct career path:
1. Are you having fun yet?
2. Do you look forward to going to work?
3. Are you proud of what you are doing?

If you realize that you are in the wrong profession, change. Life is too short to stagnate in a frustrating career.

COMMITMENT. Successful individuals put themselves on the line—they pour all of themselves into a project. They realize that failure doesn't count; persistence does. Hank Aaron struck out more than any other major league baseball player; he also hit more home runs. If you view failure as a learning technique for success and you persist despite setbacks, you are committed and you will inevitably succeed. Life is filled with disappointments and problems but those who learn from their conflicts can come back stronger than ever. Indeed, a crisis is an opportunity for growth.

DEFINITE FOCUS. Successful people set priorities and learn to focus. They work on what they do best and do the most important things first. Those that focus well report a combination of physical relaxation and increased mental alertness when they are concentrating on a project. To stay focused, ask yourself, "What's the best use of my time right now?"

CONFLICT-FREE. Unconscious psychological conflicts can prevent success. If you are anxious or depressed most of the time or if you have multiple physical complaints—headaches, stomachaches, back pain, etc.—or if every work project seems to fail, you probably have unconscious psychological problems contributing to your difficulties. These barriers are difficult to remove because they are hidden and to understand them requires reflective thinking. Your best friends may be able to help you see the reason for your difficulties before you do. Ask them!

GOOD LUCK. Good fortune seems to shine on successful people. Success breeds success and winners have a habit of winning. These aphorisms are crucial to understanding success. They indicate that if you can become in some small way successful, then little by little you will begin to feel lucky, and the more you think of yourself as being lucky, the luckier you will become. Optimism breeds good fortune. ✖

...Noble Spirits Make

Finding Value In A Duck Blind

When I was a young lad, but old enough to know better, I held the bag on a snipe hunt. My fellow Boy Scouts on an overnight camping trip told me that the snipes flew low and could be caught in a bag if the hunter positioned himself in a corner of a field between two tall trees. Because you could not hear the snipes coming, they said, you must hold the bag wide open. It took patience and a steady hand to be a good snipe hunter.

Finding the appropriate area at the edge of a field, my companions left me, they said, to drive the snipes across the field and into the bag. Assuming a comfortable position next to one of the trees, I held the bag wide open for a considerable time, but nothing flew in. Finally, puzzling over why my companions had failed to let me know that they had given up, I marched back toward the campfire. As I approached the firelight, I became the source of gleeful entertainment for my friends cozily roasting marshmallows. I am the only person I know who ever held a snipe bag.

Over three decades later my continued reputation for naivete and gullibility must have led to my being invited on a duck hunt during the coldest weekend of the year. The weather was bitterly cold; temperatures hovered around freezing. A fine mist, alternating with icy sleet, was falling. The blast of cold north wind howling over the water produced an arctic chill factor.

My companions, experienced hunters all, were well insulated, rubberized, waterproofed, and camouflaged in their L.L. Bean and Cabella outfits. One had a coat with enough pockets to make the Artful Dodger dizzy with ecstasy. He had a place for Kleenex, another pocket for a camera, another for lip balm and hand cream, a pocket for shells, and a pocket for a medicinal to clear his sinuses and warm his insides. Dressed in his coat, he was a walking U-Haul Trailer.

All but me were dressed so appropriately that I fully expected the ducks flying over their blind to drop dead from fear, knowing that they were about to meet the shells fired by the best hunters in Texas.

I, in contrast, put on a motley combination of under-shirts, ski clothes, and coveralls so bulky that I walked like C-3PO. Even with all of that gear, I became a 6'3" icicle as our duck-blind-bound airboat moved swiftly through the arctic air.

Arriving at my blind, I found the moist seat saturated my non-waterproof pants while my feet quickly numbed in the four inches of water. The freezing weather, combined with my bulky clothes, frozen fingers, runny nose, poor aim, and my remembrance of Matthew 10:29 ("Are not sparrows sold for penny? Yet not one of them will fall to the ground apart from the will of your Father") made it perfectly safe for the ducks to fly over me. Seeing the outlandish outfit of an obviously inexperienced hunter, the ducks appeared peacefully secure as they circled my blind like buzzards.

As I sat in the windblown, water-soaked blind, I kept asking myself, "Am I having fun yet?" And, the answer always came out an astounding, "Yes," but I couldn't understand why. Later, when my friends were asked what they enjoyed about duck hunting, they said things like, "It's nice to get away with the other guys," "It's fun to get back to nature again," "It helps develop survivor skills." All these answers were true, but there appeared to be a deeper reason also. Life is simpler in the duck blind and, for a few hours, we forget our worries.

In our group were bankers, insurance agents, physicians, attorneys, entrepreneurs, and businessmen. There was much laughter and good-natured kidding in our group, but beyond the happiness, one could sense a nostalgia for a simpler life. During more contemplative times, we talked of increasing insurance rates, the unstable economy, government regulations, our litigious society, the fluctuating stock market, rising health costs, the AIDS dilemma and the drug abuse problem. All of us were boys grown old, perplexed by a troubled world.

As we drove home, I wondered what we returning hunters could do to help our country overcome some of its problems. Although we cannot control others, we can, ourselves, practice integrity and honesty. We can give a hard day's work for a fair day's pay. We can simplify our lives. We can stand for goodness and truth. We can elect officials who are willing to help lead the country to basic decency. We can refuse to tolerate laziness, greed, and immorality.

Long ago I sat innocently hopeful, holding a snipe bag. No longer innocent, but hopeful still, I am convinced that compassion and sacrifice will prevail. Being with my friends, noble citizens all, reaffirmed my belief that our country's people can endure society's trying times.

It's A *Wonderful* Life

⌘

The misty, cold weather we had for Thanksgiving made the day especially fine for fireplace and family. After the turkey was carved and prayers were said, I announced to my wife's sister and her family who had joined us that all would take turns giving thanks for those things we most appreciated.

We would make the circuit around the table three times telling what we were thankful for; no one could repeat what anyone else had said. It sounds mawkishly sentimental, but it worked. We all felt closer and better understood. I was pleased that we were all grateful for meaningful things. No one expressed thanks for their cosmetics, cash, or cars.

I also discovered that my brother-in-law could speak eloquently and lengthily on the value of love and family. No wonder my children give me grief over my discourses and harangues. He had some good points, though, and I made copious notes. I'm always looking for fresh material.

After dinner, my brother-in-law, tired by his speech-making, slept while the rest of us teamed up to play Pictionary. Ours was a typical Thanksgiving Day duplicated by thousands of other families, but nonetheless deeply meaningful and richly satisfying.

Later after the dishes were washed and the relatives waved happily home, my daughter and I had a magical time together that, because of its simplicity, I will always remember. I put a couple of logs on the fire and, my daughter and I sat silently together gazing into the flames for many minutes.

I thought of next year when she would be off to college and reflected on how special she had always been and how much I loved her. Always a deep thinker, mature and understanding, she is much more advanced than I was at seventeen.

I thought of all the years I had wasted on superfluous things and that only recently, despite years of training, education, and experience, had I begun to realize what makes life significant. We can find meaning only by cultivating love, wisdom, peace of mind, faith, and joy. Strengthened with these virtues, life becomes simpler and many things that used to matter greatly are no longer troublesome. The task, now, becomes to refine these virtues and through example, teach them to others.

Frank Kapra's 1946 movie, It's a Wonderful Life, starring Jimmy Stewart, illustrates how one man's simple acts of kindness can influence the entire community. On the verge of suicide, George Bailey, the protagonist is shown by his guardian angel, Clarence, what the world would have been like if he had not lived. George learns that "...each man's life touches many others and when he isn't around, it leaves a terrible hole."

Because we have lived, the world is different.

How can we become more loving? To love requires that we give up self-centeredness. This task is a constant struggle. Television ads, movies, newspapers and magazines emphasize self-absorption. It's necessary, of course, to love ourselves as children of God and to let our good works shine for the benefit of others. To be only concerned about our individual desires, however, is detrimental to our emotional and spiritual growth.

If we live with love, the world will be much more loving because our kind deeds influence many others to act with love. We must aim to live our lives so that others will be happy to see us. We ought to try to live so that when we walk into a room, the people in it will feel better because we are there.

Wisdom comes from education and experience to those who study and reflect. With wisdom, we find that every failure, every disappointment, every conflict brings benefit and opportunity for growth and improvement. We learn from our mistakes and our successes.

Peace of mind comes when we understand that, as King Arthur says in Camelot, each of us is "...just a tiny drop in the great blue ocean of the sunlit sea, but some of the drops do sparkle." We gain peace of mind when we know God's purpose for us. That purpose will make our insignificant existence significant and we will sparkle with enthusiasm and energy.

Faith means that we need not worry. There is a good plan for all of us. God will direct us to that correct path if we take time to listen, really listen.

Joy comes from becoming more childlike. To be joy-ful means that we must drop the facade. We must stop being pretentious, stop trying to act as if we are what we are not, and have fun being alive.

This holiday season we must take time to reflect on the true values of life. In our frantic rush of parties and gift-buying, let's take time for love, wisdom, peace of mind, faith, and joy.

Great To Be An American

Summer, the time for soft sleepy ease, green grass, kids-out-of-school, and baseball, can best be remembered for vacations. A working vacation I took last year summons up special memories this Independence Day weekend.

I had been asked to present a series of lectures on psychosomatic medicine to the First Brazilian Conference on Psychiatry and Medicine held in Sao Paulo, Brazil. The 575 physicians attending the Congress received my lectures via simultaneous translation. The Brazilian interpreters asked me to speak slower than usual, but I soon forgot their request until I noticed the two interpreters in their glass booth alternately fanning each other and drinking copious amounts of water. I slowed then and consequently the audience started laughing at my jokes on cue. It's nice to know that what's funny in Lufkin, Texas, also goes over in the largest city in South America.

Between lectures my doctor friends gave me a tour of the city. My chief guide, a professor at the medical school, had difficulty speaking English and driving at the same time and therefore did both very poorly, but with marked enthusiasm. The other drivers were just as enthusiastic and had mastered Portugese expletives so that my trips through the city were just as entertaining and colorful as any ride I've experienced at Six Flags. We toured museums, universities, parks, and the largest snake farm in Latin America, with more than 70,000 snakes in its collection. Antitoxin extracted here is sent all over the world.

Here are some things I learned on my trip. The Brazilian restaurants specialize in grilled squid. A barbecue is a steak house. The beer is flat and the coffee bitter. The Brazilian people are addicted to soccer and the television carries mostly American reruns, very old reruns. Sao Paolo has grandly-built universities, but not many books. Crime is rampant.

Of the 14 million people living in Sao Paulo, 4 million are abandonded children. The hotel doorman, a highly intelligent individual knowledgeable in international politics and graced with a command of English, French, Portugese, and German, told me that crime was out of control, the people were starving and the police corrupt. Of a tour group of forty staying in my hotel, ten had been mugged and robbed.

The most memorable part of the trip was a visit to The Hospital de Clinicas, the medical school hospital, the primary referral hospital for all Brazil. A tour of the general hospital emergency room reminded me of the railroad yard scene from GONE WITH THE WIND. There were patients lying on stretchers in the corridors and anteroom of the ER complex, dozens of them, all with horrible injuries or illnesses—gunshot wounds, accidents, stabbings, pneumonias, exotic Amazon fungal diseases, alcohol withdrawal syndromes, bleeding ulcers. As I walked through corridor upon corridor and room after room, I was reminded of the verses from Matthew 9:34-36, "And what pity he felt for them, because their problems were many and they had not a place to go or anyone to help. They were like sheep without a shepherd."

A young intern in charge of treating this mass of humanity, the most remarkable man I met on my trip, said, "Doctor, how do you like our PLATOON? You have seen the movie? Well, here it is, in 3-D. What can I do—except the best I can?" His beaming cheerfulness that belied the hopelessness of the situation was the only morphine the rows and rows of vacant-eyed, suffering patients got that day, but what a powerful dose!

I learned many lessons on my Brazilian trip. Most important, I learned it's great to be an American. This Independence Day, sitting on the lawn with my friends, watching the Fourth of July fireworks in the park below, I'll think back on my trip to Brazil and thank God I was born here and that I'm a country boy and that life for us is good.

A *Time For All Things*

Rain had interrupted the golf game, and so our foursome, as groups are apt to do when given a few idle minutes, ruminated on things past. Someone mentioned how swiftly time flew. "It seems that the clocks run faster every day and the months don't last as long on the calendar," he said. Someone else suggested that attention to time is one indication of greatness: those acutely aware of the brevity of life tend to accomplish more with their allotted time.

Our resident Shakespearian scholar mentioned that one of the recurring themes of Shakespeare's sonnets is time. Shakespeare," he said, "wrote frequently about how time steals away youth." To prove his point he began to quote "Sonnet 15," "Where wasteful time debateth with decay, to change your day of youth to sullied night." In "Sonnet 16," "Make war upon this bloody tyrant, Time." In "Sonnet 65," "What strong hand can hold [Time's] swift foot back?"

When he began "Sonnet 30" our group disbanded. Nothing breaks up a good bull session faster than quoting Shakespeare. Later I began to think about some of the ideas our conversation generated. Most of us don't use our time wisely. That is why we so desperately miss it when it is gone. Here are some thoughts on how to better use time:

SET PRIORITIES. Do the most important things first. For some unexplained reason, we seem to spend most of our time on low value activities. We get bogged down on second and third-rate activities instead of spending time on the important tasks. To counteract this bad habit, make a list each morning of the things to be accomplished, number them and do them in the order of their importance.

CONTROL YOUR ALLOTMENT OF TIME. Fill your calendar with those activities that are important to you. When someone calls you can tell them, truthfully, that you don't have time in your schedule for their committee meeting. My secretaries schedule I. B. Quiet on my appointment book from 3:00 until 3:30 every afternoon; this gives me time to rest and refresh my mind each day.

KNOW YOUR RHYTHMS OF MAXIMUM EFFECTIVE-NESS. Some people are early morning people; others are late evening people. Some people work better in the winter; others work better in the summer. By understanding your rhythms you can use the time that you are at your best to do those things that are most important to you and your career. Perhaps early in the week is the best time for you to work on projects, whereas the latter part of the week is best for committee meetings, public relations, or independent study. Summer might be the best time for catching up on your reading, while fall and winter may be best for you to work harder on developing your business.

LEARN TO SAY NO. You must say "NO" to insignificant projects to be able to say "YES" to things of lasting value. There are many ways to say "NO." "That's a great project but it's something that I know very little about. I'm afraid that I am going to have to decline." Or, "That's a worthy project but it doesn't fit into my time schedule." If you don't protect your allotment of time, no one else will.

REMEMBER THE OBVIOUS. Schedule time for spiritual growth; otherwise you will neglect one of life's most important disciplines. Disorganized people rarely enjoy intimacy with God. Time must be set aside for Bible study, prayer, worship, and meditation.

Establish definite family time. Make every effort to have breakfast and dinner with the entire family. Put your son's basketball game and your daughter's dance recital on your calendar. Take one evening a week to dine out with your wife or husband; take one weekend a month to get away with your spouse.

Neglecting study is easy. If you don't study, you don't get smart. If you don't get smart, you don't improve. If you don't improve, you may find your business deteriorating and yourself becoming stagnant. Read for thirty minutes each evening.

ESTABLISH TIME FOR REST. Know your limits. Rest and relax to gather inner strength. Make Sunday a day of rest.

The Old Testament book, *Ecclesiastes*, takes a reassuring view of time: "For everything there is a season, and a time for every matter under heaven. A time to be born, and a time to die; a time to plant, and a time to harvest; a time to weep, and a time to laugh." Solomon, in Ecclesiastes, thus indicates that if we have proper perspective, there is little need to mourn time's passing.

The Ennobled Soul

⌘

Many summers ago, one of my mentors at Duke told me, "To be a good psychiatrist requires an understanding of psychodynamics, social systems, family structure, neurochemistry, and interpersonal conflicts; but in the final assessment, love answers all life's problems. Love is the balm that heals all wounds."

More words have been written on love than any other emotion. Poets extol it; psychologists explain it. Love is the thread that ties together all great novels and stories. Philosophers write of romantic and platonic love, but to others there are three types of love: love of God, love of self, and love of others.

LOVE OF GOD. The classic joke tells of a man clinging to the edge of a cliff by a bush that is gradually pulling away from the mountainside. The man yells, "Help, help. Is there anyone up there to help me?" Out of the clear blue sky comes a booming voice, "Yes, my son, this is the Lord God Almighty. I will help you if you believe in me. Do you believe in me?" The man replies, "Yes, Lord, I believe in you!" God then says, "If you believe in me, let go of that bush." The man quickly yells, "Help, help. Is there anybody else up there?"

For most of us, love of God means turning to Him when we are in trouble. And even then we have our doubts. We may do nothing to cultivate a relationship with God until tragedy strikes and then suddenly begin to ask God for help. Our faith is weak, however, if we have no permanent relationship with Him.

To cultivate a meaningful relationship with God requires daily meditation and scriptural study. A solid relationship with God can be maintained only through daily prayer. "But when you pray, go into your room and shut the door and pray to your Father who is in secret; and your Father who sees in secret will reward you." (Matthew 6:6).

A loving relationship with God enables us to tolerate the stresses of life and overcome them. "Do not be conformed to this world but be transformed by the renewal of your mind, that you may prove what is the will of God, what is good and acceptable and perfect." (Romans 12:2). Paul reminds us, "Have no anxiety about anything, but in everything by prayer and supplication with thanksgiving let your request be known to God." (Phillipians 4:6).

With daily time devoted to prayer we establish priorities. Daily prayer enables us to realize that God's peace is always with us and enables us to feel loved and, in turn, to love more abundantly. Prayer resembles recharging a battery. We are recharged with love every time we pray.

SELF-LOVE. Prayer also enables us to learn to love ourselves appropriately. Unfortunately, few of us truly

love ourselves. Many of us believe that to love ourselves is a sin. We confuse self-love with self-
absorption. Pride and self-absorption restrict our emotional growth and diminish our capacity to relate
warmly to others. Self-love, however, enables us to love
others better and to become a productive force in the
universe.

In Corinthians 3:16, Paul writes, "Do you not know
that you are God's temple and that God's spirit dwells
within you." If God's spirit dwells in us, then to love
God we must love ourselves. People who love themselves reflect God's love to others without conditions.

Self-love means accepting our limitations and
developing our talents. Jesus tells us, "Let your light
so shine that men may see your good works and give
glory to your Father who is in Heaven" (Matthew 5:16).
We do not want to keep our light under a bushel.
We want our light to shine forth abundantly.

Self-love also means protecting our time and not
allowing others to use us or abuse us. Self-love means
becoming a doorway for others, not a doormat.

If we love ourselves and avoid laziness, we develop
our talents. We work on spreading patience, goodwill,
care, cheer and joy.

LOVE OF OTHERS. In the Sermon on the Mount
Jesus said, "But I say to you, love your enemies and
pray for those who persecute you, so that you may
be sons of your Father who is in Heaven."

In Les Miserables, Victor Hugo gives an example of
brotherly love. Jean Valjean, released from prison after

nineteen years as a galley slave, was refused lodging repeatedly because his yellow passport identified him as an ex-convict. Finally, the Bishop of Digne kindly invited him to spend the night at his home. During the night, Jean fled with the Bishop's silverware. The police found Jean Valjean with the silver and returned him to the Bishop for identification. Much to Valjean's surprise, the priest told the police that he had given the silverware to Jean Valjean and urged Valjean to take the silver candlesticks that he had forgotten. Puzzled, the police let the prisoner go.

When they were alone the Bishop told Jean Valjean, "You no longer belong to evil, but to good. I have bought your soul for you. I withdraw it from black thoughts and the spirit of perdition, and give it to God." The Bishop's kindness transformed Jean Valjean from a bitter criminal to a man of love. Jean Valjean began to love others as he had been loved by the Bishop. In loving others Valjean found sainthood.

As Emmet Fox said in *The Sermon on the Mount*, "There is no difficulty that enough love will not conquer; no disease that enough love will not heal; no door that enough love will not open; no gulf that enough love will not bridge; no wall that enough love will not throw down; no sin that enough love will not redeem ... If only you could love enough you would be the happiest and the most powerful being in the world."

The Inward-Dwelling Spirit

✄

Before we can love others, we must love ourselves. Self-love is not narcissism. It is not asking the mirror, "Who is the fairest of them all?" Self-love is not thinking of ourselves to the exclusion of others. It is not the pursuit of wealth, power and beauty.

Self-love means accepting our limitations and appreciating our talents. "Do you not know that you are God's temple and God's spirit dwells in you?" (I Cor. 3:16). If our bodies represent the temple of God, then our bodies are worth taking care of; if God's spirit dwells in us, then we are responsible for allowing that spirit to develop to the fullest. Self-love, then, means taking care of our bodies, accepting our limitations, and striving to grow emotionally, intellectually, and spiritually.

ACCEPTING OUR LIMITATIONS. Recently, a friend's son became dejected because he had played a poor game of basketball. The boy made a couple of poor passes, missed some easy shots, and failed to block out when rebounding. The coach pulled him from the game. The following game the boy had no confidence. He hesitated to shoot and was reluctant to pass the ball. He looked scared and insecure.

My friend wisely talked to his son. He told him, "Everybody makes mistakes. No one is perfect. The important part of playing basketball is to give it all you've got. If you are not giving it all you've got, you are cheating yourself and your teammates. Champions always keep trying."

He went on to tell his son, "Whether you make your shots or miss your shots, your mother and I still love you. All we want you to do is to shoot joyfully and play with enthusiasm." The following game, the boy scored fourteen points but, more importantly, he played with enthusiasm and confidence.

Self-love, then, is refusing to get down on ourselves. Discouragement limits our potential. Learn from our mistakes, yes. Seek forgiveness, yes. But then get on with it. Otherwise, we become morose, gloomy, depressed. We are good for no one, least of all ourselves. We are cursing God's temple.

Unfortunately, many people go through life unwilling to accept that they are not perfect. In their frenetic drive to do everything right, they miss the spontaneity of living. They become self-absorbed, but they don't love themselves.

TAKING CARE OF OUR BODIES. If we love ourselves, we take care of our bodies. We maintain proper weight, practice regular physical exercise, get the proper amount of rest and relaxation, avoid cigarettes, and limit our alcohol intake.

INTELLECTUAL GROWTH. If we love ourselves, we work hard to develop not only our bodies but also our minds. We read. We study. We learn something new each day. Sir William Osler, one of the greatest minds in medicine, reported that he was not overly endowed with brilliance. He simply studied harder and longer than his colleagues. "The master word is *work*; the dull man it makes bright, the bright man brilliant, and the brilliant man steady."

If we truly love ourselves, we will develop our intellect. Often we are lazy. We prefer to gripe and complain about how fortunate other people are rather than working to improve our lot. Gripe less, read more, and our lives will be enriched.

EMOTIONAL GROWTH. We grow emotionally by working on our personalities and character structures. Part of this growth means accepting our limitations and forgiving ourselves for our faults. Growing emotionally also means respecting our feelings. We set limits on our feelings—we harness them so that our feelings work for us to provide us with the energy needed to accomplish the tasks of daily living. When we love ourselves, we avoid complaining, demanding, blaming, and ridiculing.

On the other hand, we allow our feelings to shine through in spontaneity and good will. We laugh loudly and see the joy in daily experiences. We recognize the need for affection and tenderness. We make life a joyful journey. We bring delight into relationships.

SPIRITUAL GROWTH. The ultimate in self-love is to develop ourselves spiritually, to draw closer to God. In our travel Godward, we attempt to allow all hostility, resentment, anger, frustration, and envy to drop away so that only the spirit of love remains. To allow the Kingdom of God within us to grow requires daily prayer and meditation. We actively pray for wisdom and for love, and we also set aside a few minutes every day for silence, to allow God to talk to us.

Self-love means accepting our limitations and striving to develop our full potential. Because of God's saving grace we are free to develop our full potential and reflect His love in our joyful growth.

A *Far, Far Better Thing*

A story I came across recently presents a priceless example of love and sacrifice. Colonel John W. Mansur reports in *Reader's Digest* that during the Vietnamese War several children were killed by mortar rounds which landed in an orphanage run by a missionary group. An American Navy doctor and nurse who soon arrived to administer first aid discovered that several more children were wounded, including one eight-year-old girl.

They established that the young girl, the most critically injured, would die of shock and loss of blood without quick action. To save her life, a transfusion was essential. A screening test showed that several uninjured orphans, but none of the Americans, had the matching blood type needed for an emergency transfusion.

The doctor and nurse used a combination Pidgin Vietnamese, a smattering of high school French, and impromptu sign language to explain to the young, frightened children that unless they could replace some of the girl's lost blood, she would surely die. They pleaded for someone to give blood.

After several long moments, a small boy hesitantly

raised his hand. Quickly the young boy was laid on a pallet, his arm swabbed with alcohol, and a needle inserted in his vein. After a moment of restrained silence he quickly covered his face with his free hand and let out a shuttering sob. The sobs gave way to intense, steady crying. He denied having any pain, but the American doctor and nurse were deeply concerned.

To their relief a Vietnamese nurse arrived to help. She spoke rapidly to the little one in Vietnamese and answered him in a soothing voice. Immediately, the young patient stopped crying and a look of tremendous relief spread over his face. The nurse quietly explained to the Americans, "He thought he was dying. He misunderstood you; he thought you had asked him to give all his blood so the little girl could live."

When, at the request of the Americans, the Vietnamese nurse asked the little boy why he would be willing to die he answered simply, "She's my friend." "Greater love has no man than this, that he lay down his life for a friend," (John 15:13).

In Dickens' *Tale of Two Cities*, Sydney Carton gives his life at the guillotine to save Charles Darnay, husband of Lucie Manette, whom Carton loved. Earlier Carton had solemnly assured Lucie that he would do anything for her—"I would give my life, to keep a life you love beside you!" As he marches to the guillotine, Carton sees his sacrifice justified by the happiness of Darnay and his family; for he kept his promise to Lucie to save a life dear to her. His last words are one of the most famous in literature: "It is a far, far better thing I do, than I have ever done; it is a far, far better rest I go to than I have ever known."

Most likely we will never be called to die so that others may live, but we have the opportunity to serve others daily. We can dedicate our lives to the spiritual growth of others.

Many decades before Ralph Moody published his book *Life After Life* documenting the experiences of some 150 people who had suffered cardiac death and then revived, my grandmother told a similar story. Long ago when she was a mother of five small children, my grandmother was stung by a bee. Terribly allergic to bee stings, she died. She felt her spirit floating up out of her body and could see herself lying on the ground, the family gathering around her.

Her spirit was then transported rapidly through a dark tunnel at the end of which was a brilliant, peace-giving light. As her spirit approached this all-encompassing light, she felt completely peaceful. A spirit figure that she perceived to be God communicated with her. This god-like spirit stressed two things about her life—how she had loved and what she had learned.

She asked the peace-giving spirit to allow her to return to earth to take care of her five small children. Next, she remembered awakening in a tub with my grandfather's mother splashing cold water over her.

This life-after-death experience profoundly affected

my grandmother. Always kind and gentle, she became saint-like. Throughout her life she continued to be one of the most loving and benevolent individuals I have ever met.

It is unnecessary to serve heroically to serve well. The small good grace that we demonstrate to others is as significant as a lofty demonstration of benevolence. Kindness is infectious. Love answers all problems.

Reflections On Love

�֍

Now marks the time to reflect on love—its meaning and significance in this world of war, terrorism, destruction, and mayhem. In this world one out of five people has a major mental disorder, almost half of the marriages end in divorce, nearly two-thirds of all high school seniors have used an illicit drug at least once, one out of ten people is alcoholic, and a violent crime is committed every ten seconds. What is the answer to all this chaos? The only answer is love.

Love does not demand or control. Love does not give unwisely or nurture destructively. It is not self—sacrifice. Although love can be romantic, it is not simply romance. Although love can be sensual, it is much more than sexual desire. Love is not proud or boastful. It is not rude or inconsiderate.

Love is kind. Love is loyal. Love is trusting. Love endures. Love brings peace of mind. Love always wins.

M. Scott Peck, M.D., in his extraordinary book, *The Road Less Traveled*, defines love as, "The will to extend one's self for the purpose of nurturing another's spiritual growth." Love allows us to grow spiritually, emotionally, and intellectually. And, through our loving those around us, we evolve into more loving individuals so that love is an ever-expanding circular process. Just as we cannot be a source of strength unless we are strong, we cannot love others unless we first love ourselves. To love, then, means that we are dedicated to our own development as well as the development of others. We can love only through effort and will. Love is desire willed into action. Peck expands on the following points:

LOVE REQUIRES ATTENTION. When we love another person, we give that person our attention. We attend to that person's emotional, physical, spiritual, or mental growth. We pay attention by listening. Really listening is hard work and requires effort and concentration. How many of us really listen to what our children, our spouses, our parents, our friends, our customers say to us? Really listening means that we must weigh each word and understand each sentence.

LOVE REQUIRES RISK. Love means moving out to another human being and risking rejection. We can elect to isolate ourselves from others, to stay the same, and to keep the same circle of friends. It takes courage to reach out to a stranger or a new neighbor, but, as with any risk, there is always the opportunity of great reward.

There is also the risk of growing up—the act of stepping from childhood to adulthood. Growing up means making free choices and refusing conformity.

LOVE REQUIRES TRUTH. All evil begins with a lie. We lie to ourselves when we drink too much. We lie when we cheat on an examination. We lie when we don't do our best at work. To love means that we are totally and completely honest with ourselves and with others.

Shakespeare's admonition, "To thine own self be true, and it must follow as the night the day, thou canst not then be false to any man," has been quoted so often it has almost become a cliche. Nevertheless, this is one of the most powerful statements in all literature. Love cannot exist without the truth and the truth allows us to be totally free to reach our fullest potential and to enable others to reach theirs.

LOVE REQUIRES COMMITMENT. Love means making a commitment to the nurturing of someone else. Loyalty and commitment foster the growth of ourselves and others. When a loved one wrongs us, we forgive. We accept imperfection.

LOVE REQUIRES CONFRONTATION. When we love someone, we take the risk of confronting them. We are not afraid to tell them that they have gone astray. As parents, teachers, leaders, we exercise power. We take the awesome responsibility of influencing and shaping others. When we confront, it must be done with a humble spirit, for we, too, are imperfect.

LOVE IS DISCIPLINED. We can elect to set no limits on our loved ones, provide no direction, fail to make clear who leads. Or, we can maintain rigid control. Proper discipline requires finding the balanced middle path, a task which requires constant judgment and continuing adjustment. We listen to our children, but we also limit them. We redirect them and teach them.

We maintain a healthy self-discipline that models good behavior.

LOVE IS SEPARATENESS. The genuine lover always allows the beloved to have a totally separate identity. Love requires that we appreciate the unique individuality of our loved ones and not view them as extensions of ourselves. To paraphrase Kahlil Gibran, we are the bows from which others, as living arrows, are sent forth. Your purpose is to help your loved ones grow to be the most they can be, not for your benefit, but for their own.

Christmas Spirit

✼

O. Henry's classic, *The Gift of the Magi*, tells of Della and Jim, who forced by poverty, sold their most precious possessions on Christmas Eve. Della sold her beautiful hair "...rippling and shining like a cascade of brown waters" to buy a platinum fob chain for her husband Jim's watch; while Jim, "...only 22 and in need of a new overcoat and without gloves", sold his only treasure, a gold watch that had been his father's and his grandfather's, to buy an elegant set of combs for Della to wear in her beautiful hair.

O. Henry concludes the story, "The magi, as you know, were wise men—wonderfully wise men—who brought gifts to the Babe in the manger. They invented the art of giving Christmas presents. And here I have lamely related to you the uneventful chronicle of two foolish children in a flat who most unwisely sacrificed for each other the greatest treasures of their house. But in a last word to the wise of these days let it be said that of all who give gifts, these two were the wisest. Of all who give and receive gifts, such as they are wisest. They are the magi."

Reading *The Gift of the Magi* reminds me of my mother's gift. Poverty-stricken also, she sacrificed daily so that her sons could have the best she could provide. The meager material possessions she gave us were insignificant compared to the persistent encouragement, hope, and emotional warmth that she provided. Although daily burdened with financial worries, our mother, nonetheless, never let us know how precarious our situation was. Instead, she endured alone, providing us emotional security, which is far more valuable than any material gift. Hers was a gift of the magi.

The question for this Christmas and all Christmases to come, is, "How can we be magi?" How can we, amidst the frantic rush and crush of Christmas, be wise enough to take time to give the gifts that endure forever?

In our country, the wealthiest of all nations of all time, people live in squalor and poverty. There are those who sleep in cardboard box houses; some must rely on sparse government checks for sustenance; others wander from place to place in search of handouts and home. On Christmas Day our television sets will show lines of people receiving turkey dinner from the Salvation Army. We will view the alleyways of the destitute and the poor.

Pity them, but pity more the vast army of people who are rich in possessions, but poor in spirit. Pity the owners of all imaginable material possessions— those wearers of Rolexes and drivers of Cadillacs who feel emotionally empty. Pity those who have so much luxury that their greed becomes insatiable and they must ply themselves with cocaine to have a moment of euphoria. Pity those, for they have no love, no wisdom, no serenity.

Give us this Christmas the hope that the world can return to the basic virtues that endure and give life meaning. Let us look to what is valuable. Let us be grateful for the gift of being able to give. Let us be thankful for love, wisdom, faith, serenity, and joy.

Let us have the Christmas of Bob Cratchit in Dickens' A *Christmas Carol*, who said, "There are many things from which I might have derived good, but from which I have never profited, Christmas among the rest. But I am sure I have always thought of Christmas time, when it has come round—apart from the veneration due to its sacred name and origin, if anything belonging to it can be apart from that—as a good time; a kind, forgiving, charitable, pleasant time; the only time I know of, in the long calendar of the year, when men and women seem by one consent to open their shut-up hearts freely, and to think of people below them as if they really were fellow passengers to the grave, and not another race of creatures bound on other journeys. And therefore, though it has never put a scrap of gold or silver in my pocket, I believe that it has done me good, and will do me good; and I say, God bless it!"

Let it be said of us that we ·know how to keep Christmas well—that we receive gratefully and give lovingly; that our hearts fill with laughter and our eyes sparkle with joy; that we love tenderly and live heartily;

that we build fond memories of family and fellowship; that we take time for rest and renewal. May that we truly lived be truly said of us all. And may God bless us, everyone!

Traveling Godward

In *The Road Less Traveled* Scott Peck reminds us, "The divine intent is that we travel Godward." This simple statement inspires deep thought. In our travel Godward we can easily stumble into side paths and dead-ends. But with self-reflection, prayer, meditation, and divine guidance, we are redirected to the path that leads to life.

All great literature describes the journey Godward. Great music conveys that journey. Visual art illustrates that journey. The *Holy Bible* is the travel manual for the journey. For many, psychotherapy is the beginning of that journey.

MUSIC. Who can listen to classical music or the musical scores from *Chariots of Fire, Rocky, Out of Africa,* and *The Natural* and not be inspired to love and good works? *Beethoven's 5th Symphony* portrays the power of God in our lives. Three G's followed by an E flat (da, da, da, dumm) represents death knocking on the door and leads on to the majestic third movement that portrays the triumph of good over adversity. *Beethoven's 9th Symphony* ends with the majestic chorus, "Joyful, Joyful, We Adore Thee." Pachelbel's *Canon in D Major* reflects God's continual, persistent love. The music of Vivaldi,

Handel, and Bach reflects God's presence in our lives.

VISUAL ART. Classical paintings cause us to reflect on the divine influence in our lives. Da Vinci's *Mona Lisa*, Andrew Wyeth's *Christina's World*, and Van Gogh's *Starry Night* all fill us with the wonder of God's love. The realistic paintings of Norman Rockwell reflect the love and spirit of God in our daily lives.

PSYCHOTHERAPY. All meaningful psychotherapy is God-directed. Some patients have a view of God that restricts their Godward journey. All churches are not good; *i.e.*, some churches are destructively dogmatic and restrict an individual's spiritual growth. Some people in churches are evil; *i.e.*, there are hypocrites, liars, seducers, and manipulators who lead patients away from God. Some churches emphasize social activities to the exclusion of spiritual growth. Rigid, restrictive churches refuse to emphasize God's redeeming love and abiding, ever-present grace. Patients who come from these churches are guilt-ridden and frightened. They need to learn, through psychotherapy, of God's encouraging love.

Other patients turn away from God because they have never felt loved. Many of these patients could be classified as "poor little rich kids." They have been given material wealth but have received no true love and concern from their parents. These people are empty, lonely, and sad. They learn through psychotherapy that they are lovable and that God's spirit dwells in them. When patients are capable of recognizing the love and goodness within them, they turn to a spiritual path.

The third type of patient has given up on God. Often tragedy—a death in the family, severe business loss, unexplained disaster—has turned them away from God. Through psychotherapy they learn about the mystery of life and death, of creation and decay. They see the power of God's regeneration and renewal. They learn that miracles abound and that God's grace is abundant in all aspects of life and death.

LITERATURE. All enduring literature describes the struggle between good and evil. This description enables us to move closer toward God. Dante's *The Divine Comedy* is an excellent example of the trip Godward. *The Divine Comedy* can be understood on four levels: narrative, allegorical, moral, and mystical.

Taken narratively the epic poem describes Dante's journey through hell and purgatory toward the divine light. The book begins, "Midway through life I came to myself lost in a dark wood where the straight way was lost." Dante meets Virgil who leads him through hell.

The first five levels of hell consist of those people who sinned in the flesh (lust, seduction, gluttony, greed, and wrath). At the sixth level are the heretics; the seventh level includes suicides, blasphemers, and sexual perverts. At the eighth level are sorcerers, hypocrites, thieves, liars, and evil counselors. At the ninth level are the traitors. Frozen in the center of the earth is Lucifer.

Virgil then leads Dante through purgatory. Here Dante discusses the seven deadly sins: pride, envy, anger (representing perversions of man's instinct to love God), sloth (failure to pursue God's love), avarice, gluttony, and lust (sins that lead us away from God).

Finally, at heaven's gate Virgil turns Dante over to Beatrice (Dante's life-long love). Beatrice leads Dante through nine concentric heavens to the divine light of God.

Allegorically, *The Divine Comedy* can be understood as a metaphor for life's journey as it portrays the temptations and sins that we must overcome before we meet the divine light. In another way, *The Divine Comedy* is a metaphorical example of psychotherapy. Virgil (the psychotherapist) leads Dante (the patient) through the hell of unconscious conflicts, helps purge his sins of self-absorption, and then directs Dante toward the divine light.

Religious themes can be found in the writings of other great men of letters—Hemingway, Frost, T. S. Elliott, Flannery O'Conner, Goethe. Their writings are all worthy of deep study. Works of the arts and psychotherapy inspire us and lead us toward God.

Transcending Life's Difficulties

�֍

The opening line of Scott Peck's best seller, *The Road Less Traveled*, reads: "Life is difficult." This statement, "life is difficult," leads us, as wise statements often do, to a great paradox. When life is difficult, we tend to become very self-centered. And, often, life is difficult *because* we are too self-centered. The way out of life's difficulties is to overcome our own self-centeredness, to transcend the self, and give our lives to God. To transcend ourselves, to turn over our lives to God, to love totally, is also difficult.

How do we transcend our self-centeredness and become dedicated to God? How do we develop our spiritual capacities to the fullest?

The answer: Self-discipline. According to Peck, there are four paths of self-discipline: 1) delaying gratification; 2) accepting responsibility; 3) dedication to reality; 4) balancing.

DELAYING GRATIFICATION. Delaying gratification means putting off instantaneous pleasure to develop our talents so that we will have lasting joy. Delaying gratification to achieve spiritual, emotional and intellectual growth occurs in several ways:

* the sacrifice and hard study required for a college

or graduate education
* setting goals and working to achieve those goals
* fidelity to a commitment (i.e., keeping our promises to ourselves and others)
* prayer and meditation to strengthen our religious convictions
* psychotherapy that will help us understand and overcome our emotional weaknesses

Those who have worked for something they believe in, who have sweated and struggled to achieve a task, know that there is joy in the struggle. There is, as Robert Frost writes, "the pleasure of taking pains." Joy comes when we delay instantaneous gratification and work to become all that we are capable of being.

ACCEPTING RESPONSIBILITY. Accepting responsibility for our lives requires continual self-examination. Freedom of choice requires deep thought before deciding. Every time we make a choice, we would do well to ask ourselves, "Am I making this choice so that I can grow intellectually, emotionally and spiritually and will this choice help my loved ones grow intellectually, emotionally and spiritually?" If not, the choice is wrong.

DEDICATION TO REALITY. Dedication to reality means that we must seek a life of total devotion to the truth. As Peck points out, lying is an attempt to circumvent legitimate suffering and, hence, is productive of mental illness. We lie to ourselves and others out of a need for power, a need to be liked, or a need to protect our own sense of self-worth. There are two types of lies: a black lie, a statement we know is false; and a white lie, a statement that leaves out a significant part of the truth.

Peck gives six rules to achieve dedication to truth:
1. Never tell a black lie.
2. When truth is withheld, when a white lie is told, a significant moral decision is required.
3. Withholding the truth should never be based on personal needs, i.e., the need for power or to be liked.
4. To withhold the truth, to tell a white lie, must be based on the needs of persons from whom the truth is being withheld.
5. We should withhold the truth only when we have a genuine love for the person to whom we are telling a white lie.
6. When withholding the truth, we must ask ourselves if we help that person grow emotionally, intellectually, or spiritually by doing so.

White lies cannot be avoided in our society, but we should make certain we are telling the lie for the gain of the other person and not for ourselves.

BALANCING. Balancing, according to Peck, is assuming responsibility for ourselves and rejecting responsibility that is not truly ours. For example, we can control our thoughts and actions; we cannot control the thoughts and actions of others. Influence others, yes; control, no.

In transcending life's difficulties we are joyfully aware of God's love and grace. We gain our lives by losing our lives. We lose our lives to a God who is more powerful, more loving, more encouraging than we could ever be. As we transcend self-centeredness, life becomes less difficult.

Praying For Worthwhile Things

This week I have been listening to Wayne Dyer on audiocassette. Dr. Dyer, a marvelous speaker who has probably sold more self-help books than any other living person, gives many poignant examples on living well. In one particularly interesting vignette, he compared people with oranges. He asked rhetorically, "When you squeeze tightly on an orange, what comes out? Answer: Orange juice, of course. Why: Because that's what's inside the orange."

When you squeeze hard on people, when they are under tremendous pressure, the emotions that come out reflect their character. If you have unconscious hostility and you get under pressure, anger comes out. If you don't have the courage of your convictions and you are squeezed, frustration comes out. If you have self-doubts, anxiety comes out. If you have no purpose, depression comes out. If you're optimistic, determination comes out. If you're positive, persistence comes out. If you're happy, enthusiasm pours forth.

Recently, I have been squeezed a great deal and I don't like what's coming out—anger, doubt, tension, anxiety. I sought counsel with a good friend and spiritual advisor. Here's what he told me.

It is easy when we are under pressure to allow the negative feelings to come out if we have not been diligent about cultivating positive emotions. Life is difficult. And it's especially difficult to remain spiritual in this secular world.

My friend said that as soon as he wakes in the morning he goes into his bathroom closet and sits like a guru with his legs crossed in what meditators call the lotus position. He then begins to pray. The initial part of the prayer is one of thanksgiving. He thanks the good Lord for the day, for his health, for his loved ones, for the many opportunities and blessings that he has been given.

He then prays for his family, petitioning the Lord to help them grow emotionally, intellectually, and spiritually. He asks God to be with them daily and to give them encouragement and hope to deal with their problems.

He then asks the Lord for personal health and for love, wisdom, joy, and peace of mind. He reviews what these emotions mean. He asks for the ability to love himself—that is, to accept his limitations and develop his talents to the fullest. He asks for wisdom—i.e., to understand the other person's point of view and to weigh all the facts before making a decision. He asks that he remember throughout the day that God is guiding, protecting, and helping him. Then he asks for joy. He asks to be able to see the simple pleasures in everyday life: to appreciate the sunrise and the sunset; to let the little kindnesses in other people be appreciated; to find joy in a warm smile, a kind word, an encouraging look; and to find pleasure in health, humor, and a job well done. My friend then prays for God's spirit to grow within him so that he can show love, concern, compassion and understanding toward others.

Finally, my friend prays to keep his life on course. He knows his purpose and keeps focused on that purpose by a single-minded devotion. He asks for the achievement of certain goals that will help him accomplish his purpose in life. He prays for mastery over sin and temptation.

After prayer, my friend reads a brief devotional and a *Bible* chapter. He underlines important points and refreshes his memory of points read the previous day.

Prayer and devotion done, he leaves the house for the day's work, feeling serene and peaceful. Soon, however, with the hassles of daily living, he can quickly lose that peaceful feeling. He reports that he must constantly remind himself of his purpose and of the importance of love and the positive emotions in life. He reflects on the good by remembering what Paul wrote in Philippians 4:8, "...whatever is true, whatever is honorable, whatever is just, whatever is pure, whatever is lovely, whatever is gracious, if there is any excellence, if there is anything worthy of praise, think about these things."

With constant attention to the important issues in life we can become more joyful, more loving, and a positive influence on others. Cultivating the positive emotions—-faith, hope, love—will enable us to manage pressure with magnanimity and grace.

Our Healing Forces

According to Paul Pearsall, Ph.D., author of *Superimmunity: Master Your Emotions and Improve Your Health*, we can think ourselves healthy. "There's no longer any question that there is a link between the immune system and the brain," he says. "That means we have control over the immune system. Every thought, every feeling is accompanied by a shower of neurochemicals. It's a trip to our internal pharmacy."

The immune system, an extremely complex biochemical process, fends against diseases with antibodies formed by white blood cells. Emotionally disturbing events can disrupt the immune system, leaving us vulnerable to illnesses ranging from the common cold to cancer. Researchers studied college students for the presence of immunoglobulin that fights off respiratory infections. During exam time, there was a decrease in immunoglobulin secretion. Other studies have shown that military basic training, sleep deprivation and job stress can cause a malfunction of the immune system. Recently widowed men have increased death rates.

Evidence documenting the link between the immune system and the brain indicate the existence of two personality styles that are particularly prone to illness.

Individuals that run "hot"—those who are more impatient and take on an inordinate amount of responsibility—are more susceptible to heart disease, migraines and ulcers. "Cold" running individuals, those who feel helpless, inadequate, and victimized, seem to be more prone to cancer, arthritis and allergies. The healthy lifestyle seeks a balance between these two extremes.

Here are some ways to develop superimmunity:

LAUGH. The ability to laugh at ourselves is one of the strongest predictors of health. Today at breakfast I was berating myself for some recent foul-ups I had committed when my daughter said that my tombstone would read: "Here lies a perfectionist who didn't make it." Our good laugh helped me get a better perspective on my problems.

LOVE. Having loving relationships enhances life's good times and buffers the bad. Putting thought and energy into making relationships work is more valuable than any other endeavor. We must take time to experience God's love through prayer and devotional time. Knowing that nothing can separate us from the love of God allows us serenity and a cheerful outlook.

SIMPLIFY. Thoreau in *Walden*, published in 1854, said, "Simplify, simplify, simplify." That statement is much more true in our complex world today. The more complex we make our lives, the more difficult to maintain equanimity. To simplify, we must review our priorities daily and constantly do the most important things first.

REMAIN OPTIMISTIC. Optimism is key to good

health and a good life. The prince of optimists, Norman Vincent Peale, suggests that we adopt the "big eleven plan" and practice it every day: pray big, think big, believe big, act big, dream big, work big, give big, forgive big, love big, live big, and laugh big—and God will fill our minds with good things.

Charles Schwab, who rose from poverty to put together the United States Steel Corporation, said, "A man can succeed at almost anything for which he has unlimited enthusiasm. Any person can have enthusiasm for a few minutes, but the individual who is enthusiastic for thirty years is the one who makes a success in life."

REMAIN CALM. When we find ourselves feeling stressed out and tense we simply say to ourselves, "relax and let God." Take a deep breath in. Breathe in relaxation and breathe out tension.

LIVE POSITIVELY. Our wellness depends on our attitudes: laugh, love, dance, cheer. Health can be achieved with positive living.

As we maintain thoughts of harmony, we realize that every day is a gift from God. If we receive each day as a precious gift, we will lead physically, emotionally, and spiritually healthy lives.

Candid Camera Glasses

✼

Since the publication of *An Anatomy of an Illness* by Norman Cousins in 1979, much has been written about the use of humor in achieving physical and emotional health.

Cousins, the former editor of *Saturday Review,* discussed his bout with ankylosing spondylitis, a rheumatoid-like disorder. Considering the hospital noisy and impersonal, Cousins checked into a hotel room where he read inspirational and humorous literature and watched ''Candid Camera'' and Groucho Marx film clips. Although flat on his back with pain when the experiment began, Cousins returned to full-time work within a few months. He attributes his recovery to the cultivation of positive emotions. Humor used properly can be a beneficial antidote against the anxiety, stress, tension, and depression that contribute to physical illness.

There are three levels of humor. One detracts from good health; the other two types enhance well-being. The three types are sarcasm and self-ridicule, humor that stimulates laughter, and cosmic humor.

SARCASM AND SELF-RIDICULE. This hostile and destructive humor should be avoided at all times. If you say, "I'd rather bring my wife to the convention than kiss her good-bye," you've interfered with an opportunity for romance. If your wife says, "I've had twelve happy years of married life—not bad for eighteen years of marriage," she is unconsciously reinforcing a bad relationship. Self-denigrating remarks such as, "I don't want to belong to a club that accepts people like me as a member," will not help you overcome your negative view of yourself.

PUNS AND JOKES. Humor that provides a good laugh and is not negative can reduce anger, frustration, fear, and stress. Basically, jokes are funny because they do one of three things: 1) they overstate the truth; 2) they understate the truth; 3) they have incongruity (they have a surprise ending that adds a twist to expectancy).

Some examples of overstated humor are found in *Texas Crude: Black Humor From the Oil Patch*, compiled by Mike Cox. "Things are so tough in Big Spring, they're asking for credit references at the Dairy Queen." "What's the fastest way to become a Texas oil millionaire? Start out as a Texas billionaire." "What's the difference between the Titanic and the oil business? The Titanic had a band."

Mark Twain was a master of understatement. It was he who said, "The efficiency of our jury system is only marred by the difficulty of finding twelve men every day who don't know anything and can't read." Here's another Twain example of understated humor, "I was dangerous with a pistol, but not reliable."

Many jokes are funny because of incongruity—we expect one outcome and another is delivered. When Lou Holtz was football coach for the University of Minnesota, where the winters are particularly harsh and the children are from blond, blue-eyed Nordic stock, he said, "Minnesota is a great state with beautiful kids—they all have blond hair and blue ears."

In a speech he gave to children, Mark Twain used incongruity—he made his audience expect one outcome and then delivered another. "There are three rules to grow up with: first, don't smoke, that is don't smoke to excess; second, don't drink, that is don't drink to excess; and third, don't marry, that is don't marry to excess."

COSMIC HUMOR. Cosmic humor allows an appreciation of the paradoxes and absurdities of life. Looking at our failings in a humorous fashion allows us to be more flexible and take life in stride. With the use of cosmic humor we refuse to take ourselves and our problems too seriously.

Will Rogers said, "Friends, I don't give advice. But, if I did, I'd just say that we're only on this earth for a short time, so for heaven's sake, have a few laughs and don't take things so seriously, especially yourselves. Just live your life so you wouldn't be ashamed to sell the family parrot to the town gossip."

Here are some humor tips as suggested in *Your Emotions and Your Health*:

* Decide to be hopeful and fun-loving.
* Surround yourself with people who fill you with joy and laughter.

* Be an inverse paranoid—think the world is out to do you good.
* Put on your "Candid Camera" glasses—take 10 minutes each day to distance yourself from your environment and pretend it's all a "Candid Camera" episode.
* Read or listen to humor 5 to 10 minutes daily.
* Remember that few things are absolute or sacred—even Ann Landers got a divorce.
* Marry someone who thinks everything you say is funny.

Humor is the greatest vehicle in the world to handle the painful truth—that we are our own problems. Tell a man a joke and you have fed him for a day. Teach him to laugh at himself and you have fed him for a lifetime.

Spontaneity And A Zestful Life

⌘

Over lunch, a friend and I discussed, among other things, humor. We decided that a true wit was a marvelous but rare creature. We could name only two or three people we considered spontaneously witty individuals. I told him that the few professional comedians whom I had been privileged to meet were in no way funny off stage, but rather sober and almost reclusive.

Legend says that Bob Hope keeps five to six joke writers on call. Whenever Hope plays golf with a U. S. President or some other dignitary, he asks his joke writers for 15-20 lines that he could use—spontaneously—during the golf game. My friend reminded me that Mark Twain said, "A good ad-lib speech takes two weeks of arduous preparation."

All speakers have joke books that they review and constantly revise so they can insert fresh material into their speeches to keep the audience alert. These "zingers" or "one-liners" have been rehearsed so well they appear to be spontaneous. Almost invariably they are not. You may have observed that even the funniest person you know repeats the same gag lines.

Being witty takes practice, deep thought, preparation,

and training. Humor can, to a certain extent, be culti-
vated. We simply must be alert and train ourselves
to "think funny."

Spontaneity, too, can be developed. On my desk rest
eleven books that I have been thumbing through to
get ideas on spontaneity. That's ironic—reading
through eleven books to cultivate spontaneity. To be
spontaneous, we must allow our child-like behavior to
shine through. What makes children so attractive? Children are constantly discovering, experimenting, explor-
ing, and learning. A child is a zestful optimist—full of
wonder, risk, and trust. Unfortunately society gradually
and progressively wears away our child-like personalities.

I began thinking about this issue of spontaneity and
child-like joy when a friend recently told me that an
acquaintance who knew me in college twenty-five
years ago had described me as "a serious-minded student." Is that how I want to be remembered? A
serious-minded student? If I am to be a fully-
functioning human being who influences and shapes
the lives of others in a positive way, I must have goals
and direction but also spontaneity and child-like
warmth. If "the child is the father of the man", then I find
myself midway through life a "serious-minded adult." So
how does one cultivate spontaneity and child-like
enthusiasm? Here are some non-spontaneous thoughts:

TAKE A COSMIC VIEW OF LIFE. Sure we all have
problems, but are they really that important? We have
the problem of getting out of bed in the morning.
We have problems with our children. We have financial

problems. We are bogged down by bureaucrats and bosses. Montaigne said, "My life has been full of terrible misfortunes, most of which never happened." Worry about a problem is a bigger stress than the problem itself. We would do well to ask the question: "Is worry going to help solve the problem?" When we take the worry out of problem solving, we can make more efficient plans for defeating our difficulties.

SPREAD JOY. Moments pass swiftly and goals change. Time has little meaning without human involvement. Attempt to make every moment fresh, each relationship meaningful. Loosen up and enjoy life.

THINK FUNNY. Try to see the humor in everyday situations. Most people are trying to be something they are not. We are all pretentious and put on airs. Commercials pitch perfection—perfect bodies, perfect hair, perfect teeth. We can't be mediocre anymore. Erma Bombeck says we are made to believe that we must go through life like a miracle fabric, drip dry and wrinkle free, when we are really just trying to get from Monday to Friday in 12 days.

BUILD LEISURE INTO YOUR LIFESTYLE. Sustained effort toward a goal becomes joyless striving if not balanced by freedom, emotion and laughter. Quit work early or take time off occasionally for no real reason. Rest before you get tired. Play more; smile often. I'm going to try that too, and if it doesn't loosen me up, there are always those eleven books...

Adding Life To The Years

❀

In the 1880's when German Chancellor Otto von Bismarck set the retirement age at sixty-five, the average life expectancy was forty-five. Currently, 12% of the U.S. population (28.5 million people) are over sixty-five and by the year 2020, 17.3% will be sixty-five years or over. As Liz Carpenter, former Press Secretary to Lady Bird Johnson and author of *Getting Better All the Time*, happily concludes, "Aging has become very stylish. All the best people are doing it."

The new focus on aging is not to extend the upper limit of human life but to improve the health span—to add more life to the years. Personal habits, beliefs, and attitudes hold the key to successful aging. Active people who have faith, a purpose for living, love, and positive attitudes lead healthier, happier, and longer lives.

Studies at the Center of Aging and Human Development at Duke University Medical Center have clearly shown that people who keep active—both physically and mentally—live longer and with fewer illnesses. Just as exercising the body keeps it fit, exercising the mind keeps it functioning. Here are inspirational examples of the "use it or lose it" adage:

* At 100, Grandma Moses was painting.

* At 93, George Bernard Shaw wrote the play, "Farfetched Fables."
* At 91, Hulda Crooks had climbed 97 mountains, all of them after she turned 65.
* At 90, Pablo Picasso was producing drawings and engravings.
* At 89, Mary Baker Eddy was directing the Christian Science Church.
* At 89, Bob Hope finished a world tour for the USO.
* At 89, Albert Schweitzer headed a hospital in Africa.
* At 82, Winston Churchill wrote A History of the English Speaking Peoples.
* At 81, Johann Wolfgang von Goethe finished his play, Faust.
* At 70, Ronald Reagan was elected President of the United States.

In 1965 Leroy "Satchel" Paige, at age fifty-nine, became the oldest person to appear in a major league baseball game. Paige has strong ideas about staying youthful. Here they are:

1. Avoid fried meats which angry up the blood.
2. If your stomach disputes you, lie down and pacify it with cool thoughts.
3. Keep the juices flowing by jangling around gently as you move.
4. Go very lightly on the vices such as carrying on in society. The social ramble ain't restful.
5. Avoid running at all times.
6. Don't look back. Something might be gaining on you.

Translated, these admonitions suggest that we learn to relax, avoid worry, exercise in moderation, and eat a prudent diet.

In his book, *The Power of the Plus Factor*, ninety-year-old Norman Vincent Peale advocates cultivating the proper mental attitude. Healthy older people who sparkle with vitality and joy think of themselves as wise, experienced, emotionally mature, creative, and intelligently alert.

A satisfying, exhilarating long life requires the cultivation of a strong religious faith. Recently a major life insurance company asked policy holders who had lived to be 100 years old the most important thing they'd learned in life. "Love thy neighbor as thy self" was the most frequent answer. People who live by the golden rule experience longer and happier lives because they have diminished the deadly negative influences of anger, hatred, suspicion, jealousy, and greed that contribute to physical illness.

Belief in God restores vitality through peace of mind: "They that wait upon the Lord shall renew their strength; they shall mount up with wings as the eagles; they shall run and not be weary; and they shall walk, and not faint" (Isaiah 40:31).

Dr. Hans Selye, the father of stress research, reports that self-acceptance and living one day at a time can diminish the stress of aging. Ninety-year-old General Doolittle, who won the Congressional Medal of Honor for leading America's WWII bombing raids against Japan, suggested the reason for his long life: "I do just what I've always done. I live one day at a time."

Staying active, having something for which to live, enjoying each moment free of regret and worry, and loving God and our fellow strivers will enable us to live dynamic, healthy lives filled with joy and abundance.

The Creative Force

✳

Having been asked to speak at a fund raiser for a symphony guild, I told those gathered connoisseurs that speaking on music made me feel out of my area of expertise. I likened myself to the surgeon who came out of the operating room declaring, "Whew. That was close, two more inches and I would have been out of my specialty."

In preparing the talk I skimmed through a half dozen or more books on music. The authors of those massive tomes were futilely attempting to describe what makes music delightful—they were intellectualizing feeling. Trying to explain the value of music reminded me of what Supreme Court Justice Potter Stewart said, "I can't define pornography but I know it when I see it."

I can't define music or tell you why it's valuable, I just know that I like some music when I hear it. It seems there are two types of music. There is the music that one listens to for simple entertainment— music that makes us feel happy, or sad, or thoughtful. Then there is the highest form of music that inspires and ennobles us. The classic music, the music of masters such as Bach, Brahms, Beethoven, and Handel, inspires us to love and good works. We hear their music and recognize that man has a spirit and a soul that lives forever. Great music gives us hope, strengthens our faith, and enables us to love more completely. Great music allows us to realize the divine force within us. Music inspires us to use our full potential.

In addition, there is evidence that music may contribute to longevity. Surveys indicate that symphony conductors live longer than any other professional group. Perhaps the vigorous exercise that conductors get in the process of conducting a major symphony production, the applause and appreciation they receive from grateful audiences, and the exuberance they feel from exposure to wonderful music helps prolong their lives. Longevity may have something to do with the creative force that is within us all. If we are creatively involved in something that gives purpose and meaning, we are more likely to live long and productive lives.

Norman Cousins in his wonderful book, *The Anatomy of an Illness,* writes of his encounter with the cellist Pablo Casals. Cousins met Casals for the first time in Puerto Rico just a few weeks before his ninetieth birthday. At 8:00 a.m. his wife, Marta, helped Casals start the day. His infirmity made it difficult for Casals to dress himself; his breathing was labored, and he entered the living room on Marta's arm, badly stooped, his head pitched forward, and walking with a shuffle.

Even before eating breakfast, Casals started the day playing the piano. With discernible effort he raised his arthritic fingers to the keyboard; his back straightened and he began to breathe more freely. As he plunged into a Bach concerto, his fingers became more agile and powerful. As his body appeared infused with the music, he was no longer stiff and shrunken, but supple and graceful. Having finished the musical piece, he walked to the breakfast table straighter and taller than he had come into the room; the shuffle was gone. He talked animatedly and ate heartily.

After breakfast and an hour walk on the beach, he worked on correspondence until lunch and then napped. Cousins noticed that Casals, on awakening, was again arthritic and stiff, but as he began to play the cello, his fingers and body began to respond with controlled beauty of movement.

Cousins reported that twice in one day, he had witnessed a miracle. Music had transformed a man of almost ninety from an infirm arthritic into a temporarily healthy individual. Perhaps the creative musical performance had stimulated the production of cortisone.

If one thinks about the complex biochemical reactions of our body, creativity stimulating the production of cortisone is not a far-fetched idea. After all, when we become frightened or threatened, our body produces adrenaline that leads to high blood pressure, rapid pulse, sweating, and shortness of breath. If the negative emotions of hate, envy, anger, frustration, and resentment can cause the production of toxic neurochemical changes leading to headaches, hypertension, and ulcers, then certainly the positive emotions of love, hope, faith, and creativity can produce positive neurochemical changes that result in healthy bodies and longevity.

Life without music, life without emotion is an unlived life. Music and emotion give sweetness to our years and inspire the creative force that provides richness and depth to our lives.

...*For Wisdom Never Dies*

Father Of The Year

⌘

I didn't make it again. For the past few years I have been prompting my kids to nominate me for Father of the Year. This year I even called up their friends and asked them to send a dozen or so postcards to their favorite radio station or newspaper nominating me. I pointed out to my children and their friends all the assets that would make me an outstanding choice for Father of the Year: concern, compassion, a sense of humor, humility. But for some reason their enthusiasm for my nomination did not match mine.

When we lived in North Carolina each Father's Day the *Durham Herald* had a section featuring Fathers of the Year with articles and pictures of fathers surrounded by happy families. The chosen fathers seemed to have no problems and to be loved totally and completely by their devoted children, who evidently spent most of the time either sitting in their fathers' laps, hugging them, or gazing up at them with starry—eyed admiration. For some reason it doesn't work that way at my household. Maybe that's why I didn't get Father of the Year. I am going to keep trying though. I would appreciate it if any of you out there would be so kind as to write some postcards supporting my nomination next year. Evidently I can't count on my children to help me.

In a more serious mode, let's consider what makes a good father. Here are some thoughts:

The answer to all life's problems begins with love. Without love a father is a figurehead. A father who loves does not demand or set conditions; he's not rude or critical. He doesn't expect perfection, but, instead, accepts his child's limitations and helps the child develop his talents to the fullest. He helps his child grow emotionally, intellectually, and spiritually.

Several years ago a crucial basketball game was riding on the foul shot of a rookie player. The play-by-play announcer commented that the pressure was on the young kid to make the basket and win the game. Bill Russell, the former All-Pro performer, was doing the commentary. Russell replied, "You know I never worried about whether I made or missed free throws because I knew my father and mother would love me whether I missed them or made them." Good fathers let their children know through their words and actions that they love them whether they fail or succeed.

A loving father shows affection. He is unafraid to take his child in his arms and give a strong, comforting hug. A loving father gives pats on the back, kisses, and warm handshakes. A child can look back and remember when he struck out with the bases loaded and his father put his arm around him. Powerful, warm hugs give children security and peace of mind that they carry with them the rest of their lives.

A good father listens. He allows his children to tell their side of the story before giving advice. He pays attention to what the child is saying as well as what the child is not saying. He allows his children to ventilate criticism and encourages them to express their feelings without limitations.

Good fathers care enough to take the time to set reasonable rules and regulations. They allow their children to have a say in making the rules and, once the rules are agreed upon, they do not make exceptions to them. They stand firm and avoid being wishy-washy. They punish for breaking the rules by withholding privileges rather than striking the child or engaging in verbal abuse.

A good father models good behavior. He walks what he talks, taking great pains to have a clear conscience toward God and toward other people. He strives to grow emotionally, intellectually, and spiritually.

A good father does not take himself too seriously. He is able to accept his limitations and to realize that he is going to make mistakes. When pressure builds, he blows off steam by seeking laughter and joy. He does not ridicule his children or use sarcasm; instead, he cultivates that cosmic view of life that allows him to accept the absurdities and paradoxes found in children and others.

A good father is not always away, earning more money and propelling his career. No matter how busy he is, a good father strives to be at home for dinner and to spend at least one day a week with his children.

In listing all these virtues, I see how far short I have fallen from these goals. I am going to paste this essay on my refrigerator to remind myself of these qualities, and perhaps next year I will make Father of the Year.

How To Parent

⌘

In Shakespeare's *King Lear* are found the classic lines: "How sharper than a serpent's tooth it is to have a thankless child." All parents, from time to time, find their children ungrateful.

Human nature being what it is, I'm certain that somewhere on the past Christmas Day a child, after opening dozens of Christmas packages and finding no more under the tree, cried out, "Is this all?" The parents, having scrimped and saved to buy more gifts than they could possibly afford, wished for a tongue as rich as King Lear's so they might say, "Ingratitude, thou marble-hearted fiend, more hideous when thou show'st thee in a child."

Parents, memorize that line—"Ingratitude, thou marble-hearted fiend." You will, I'm certain, find it useful. When you buy your delightful daughter a Corvette with a 350 cc, overhead-cam, and 4-barrel carburetor and she asks, "Dad, did you fill it with gas?" You can respond, "Ingratitude, thou marble-hearted fiend."

Wise parents realize that most teenagers, most of the time, give their parents credit for almost nothing. Teenage ingratitude is a phase that parents must suffer through.

That's why I was more than pleased—I was overwhelmed with gratitude—when I recently read an essay that my teenage daughter had written about her mother and me. She said in part, "When I was younger, I looked upon my parents with awe and admiration. Upon becoming a teenager, I realized that my parents weren't perfect and could even be embarrassing. Still, they love me and try to say and do the right things...I suppose I should thank them for the things they do every day that often go unrecognized. Thanks, Mom and Dad, for everything!"

I have it in writing, folks. My daughter does appreciate us. I carry the essay in my billfold and from time to time read it. I am going to have it laminated to boost my ego, especially when she gets disgusted with my behavior. As, for example, when she reads this.

As parents, my wife and I have made many mistakes and have agonized over our child-raising decisions and confrontations. It's wonderful to know that, despite our problems, our daughter appreciates our efforts.

No parent is perfect. The best we can do is teach our children responsibility. Our children must learn that there are certain rules of society that are necessary to get along in the world and that breaking these social, ethical, and moral rules leads to self-destruction.

Here is a code for parents to try to follow in maintaining a home of good manners and simple justice:
* Praise good behavior. Catch your child doing something right and reward that behavior.
* When your child makes a mistake, correct the mistake

immediately. Let the child know why you are angry and that you expect better behavior.

* Keep the lid on your temper when things go wrong. When you lose your temper, you say things you regret later. Yelling, screaming and cursing are undignified, uncivilized and poor modeling. Anger is okay, losing your temper is not.
* Walk what you talk. Behave the way you want your children to behave.
* Be consistent in making rules and regulations. Take charge. The child feels secure when the parent shows who's boss.
* Keep your dignity and be a first class adult. Don't try to dress, dance, or talk like your kids.
* Worship together; pray together. Teach the serenity that religion gives.
* Punish the behavior, love the child. Impress on the child that lying, stealing or being cruel is intolerable.
* Don't be wishy-washy. Don't be intimidated by threats to drop out of school and leave home.
* Be honest. Always tell the truth, no matter what.

Writing these guidelines makes me realize—again—how many mistakes I've made as a parent. Being a good parent is not easy. It requires constant self-forgiveness and renewal. That's why I deeply appreciate my daughter's essay. Thanks Wende, for everything!

What Our Children Want From Us

⌘

Every Saturday morning my teenage son and I have breakfast together to talk about the past week's events. We have only two rules: I can't nag him and he can't ask me for money. We talk about happy things and generally have a good time. Several weeks ago after breakfasting on pancakes and eggs, we visited an imported car dealership to see what the rich people drive.

I've always wanted to have a Jaguar, but, because the price is about $25,000 more than I can think about paying, I, instead, go down to the Jaguar dealership and sit in one of their cars. I like to sit there, smell the leather and imagine, Walter Mitty-like, that I am driving around town in one of those luxurious automobiles. Then I remind myself that possessions don't make an individual happy and I leave the dealership smug in my conviction that I have my priorities straight.

This particular week, a fire engine red Ferrari gleamed on the showroom floor. My son and I drooled over it for a few minutes and talked with the salesman about how wonderful it would be to drive that machine. As we were leaving the showroom floor, my son folded his hands in a prayer-like gesture and jokingly pleaded, "Dad, please, please, please save up your money and get me that Ferrari. I'll never ask for anything else the rest of my life". I told him, "Brad, I can't even pronounce Ferrari much less afford to buy one. But I am glad to see you have good taste".

I then waxed philosophical. We talked about priorities and values. I asked him what traits he felt were the most important for a parent to have. Later, I sought my daughter's ideas. Here is a composite of their thoughts.

First of all, they said, a parent must be loving, and a loving parent does not hesitate to show tenderness. Good parents respect their children. Both Wende and Brad emphasized this point: "Dad, if you want us to act maturely, treat us with respect." This suggestion is a tough one. I'm afraid that if I don't guide my children, they will wander outside the white lines. Parents must master the difficult task of allowing their children enough freedom to make mistakes but enough guidance to prevent the mistakes from being big ones. We can be better parents by paying less attention to minutia and more attention to important values—love, joy, loyalty.

I am now in the "no-nag" phase of parenting. I think that's what my kids wanted when they emphasized a trusting relationship: "Treat us with respect," translates into "Don't nag." I remind them, however, that to be trusted requires trustworthy behavior. So far my "no-nag" phase works—at least my blood pressure is lower.

If we are to be good parents, we also must have good character traits. We model good behavior. If we want self-reliant children, we must ourselves be reliable. We must keep our promises to ourselves and others. Our actions must be more compelling than our words.

Good parents are also loose and forgiving. Possibly my biggest parental flaw is my intensity. I always want my children striving to excel. This intensity does nothing but upset the household. I'm a better parent when I remember the mistakes I made as a teenager. When I think back on my past, I am more forgiving of my children's mistakes.

On the other side of the coin, our children also want us to have the courage of our convictions. They want us to set reasonable rules and follow up with appropriate punishment for breaking the rules. Kids feel more comfortable when parents are strong, decisive and take charge. They want firmness and consistency.

This dichotomy of purpose is what makes parenting— and life—so difficult. It's not easy to develop a balance between rules and freedom; nor is it easy to establish a middle road between passion and prudence. That's why sitting behind the wheel of a Jaguar on the showroom floor makes me a better parent. It reminds me of my banker. He says, ''No,'' but he says it softly with compassion, empathy, and with a wistful smile of understanding.

Ties That Bind

Recently a friend told me he came home from a hard day at the office to total chaos. His wife asked what he intended to do about their rude, inconsiderate, disrespectful children who did nothing but scream at each other. He then got into a shouting match with his daughter. When the son tried to come to her rescue, another loud argument ensued. The episode left everyone smoldering and resentful.

A few hours later my friend called an emergency family conference at which time he told them that he was ashamed of the way he acted and reiterated his belief that a family should be based on love and friendship. He told his wife and children that he needed their love and support. He shared with them some of the frustrations he was experiencing at the office. His son, daughter, and wife then told him of their frustrations and resentment of his spending most of his time on his work.

The father suggested they try a new approach to family relations. He said that when he came home, he wanted a place of harmony and peace, not chaos. He said that he wanted less bickering and more love.

The next evening the family met him at the door

with exaggerated admiration and joy. His teenage son and daughter shouted with hyperbolic enthusiasm, "Oh, Dad, we are so glad to see you. You are such a nice, loving, kind, considerate father."

They led him to his favorite easy chair and helped him get comfortable. His daughter began fanning him and his son brought him the newspaper. His wife gave him a glass of Perrier and a full kiss on the mouth. They all had a big laugh together about the extravagant show of appreciation, but it did reinforce for their family that they needed to work on showing respect, concern, and compassion for each other.

My friend reports that the family still gets into occasional shouting matches. The family members, from time to time, have hurt feelings because of misunderstandings, but each time an argument occurs they remind each other that it is important to show love and respect.

Another friend called from a distant city several weeks ago. He is the director of a medical-surgical hospital, teaches at a major medical school, and has a private surgical practice. Responsibilities of the hospital, concerns about his patients, and worries about the smooth functioning of his clinic had begun to wear him down. Several of his junior partners had been complaining about inefficiency at the office and demanding that he make certain changes. His business manager and secretary were choosing sides and getting into the fracas. He asked me what he should do.

I suggested that he sit down with his key people

and share with them some of his frustrations and needs. I told him that people need to understand that efficient businesses are run on friendship and goodwill.

He called back later to say he had met with his junior partners and shared with them some of the frustrations he was experiencing. The partners shared some of their resentments and jealousies. As they talked with each other, my friend said they became aware of the need to work together and be more empathetic.

Mike Vance in his audiocassette program, "Creative Thinking" says that he once asked J. C. Penney how he put together his prosperous retail chain. Mr. Penney replied, "All great businesses are built on friendship." Sam Walton, CEO of Wal-Mart, is famous for encouraging a harmonious family atmosphere in his stores. IBM has built a multi-billion dollar business on respect for the individual.

This summer my daughter had the privilege of working in a local business office. The support and love shared there made the work enjoyable. She said the good cheer and sparkling enthusiasm that permeated the office were inspired by the owner who made specific his expectation of each employee. Good leadership can bring about synergism in an organization—where the whole is greater than the sum total of its parts." Holistic management, according to Mike Vance, "is concerned with the values of the people in the organization and with meeting their needs physically, intellectually, spiritually, and psychologically as well as financially—while developing the whole person, mind, body, and spirit.

We cannot go it alone. We need each other. A strong leader, whether in a family or in a business, needs to let the others know that harmony and goodwill are expected. Respect, friendship, and love bind organizations together.

Rainy Day Children

A few weeks ago we were getting dozens of calls at the office from frantic mothers trapped in the house with rainy day kids out of school for the summer. The mothers were crying uncontrollably; some said they were losing their minds; others reported binges of throwing dishes, pots, and pans. One mother was found slumped in the corner of the room, a blank stare on her face, a tear running down her cheek. It was a pathetic picture.

It seems that the rains are about over, but if they come again here is some advice on how to deal with rainy day children:

1) Hock your Rolex and buy a one-way ticket to Hawaii.
2) Put the kids on a Greyhound bus with a destination to their greataunt in Montana.
3) Lock yourself in the bedroom with 20 pounds of chocolates, 12 back issues of Cosmopolitan, and a dozen Neil Diamond records.
4) Go to the health club and spend 12 solid hours in the tanning booth away from all pressures and tensions.
5) Chain your children in leg irons, attach the chain

to your husband and run.

For the less adventurous, here are some reasonable ways to manage the stress of summer children and tropical rains.

One of the best ways to deal with tension is to laugh! A good belly laugh does wonders for stress. Laughing is internal jogging. Laughter shakes up the central nervous system and causes secretion of endorphins—our natural pain killers.

Don't be a slave to your children. If you are making three or four trips a day hauling them from place to place, you are traveling too much. Decide on the important functions and set limits. It is not important for them to have every video game or see every movie that they want. Your children should be expected to do a certain number of chores and to help around the house. They can also learn to keep the noise down and to have some quiet times.

When setting rules, teach your children to accept responsibility by allowing them to have a say in making the rules. Ask them to contribute their opinions on what are reasonable rules and regulations. If you disagree, try to come up with a compromise. Establish a punishment for breaking the rules and have your children agree upon it also. Remember, the best form of punishment is to withhold a privilege. Write the rules and regulations down. Have each member of the family sign the rules and paste them on the refrigerator. When the rules are broken, punishment should be immediate and should match the offense.

Remember that your children will be gone in a few short years, so learn to enjoy them and store up memories. Enjoy their wit and their personalities. Listen to them and watch them. Some of the things that irritate you now may be precious memories in the future.

You don't want to be remembered by your children as a blubbering idiot or a screaming monster; instead, you want to be remembered as a firm disciplinarian who had enough flexibility and humor to make life fun. Being a parent isn't easy but it can be fun if our priorities are straight and if we don't take ourselves too seriously.

You Can If You Will

With September just around the corner, beautifully-tanned children sunning on the beach are asking, "Why school?" This week I asked several high school students a variation of that question, "What's the main reason you go to school?" The answers varied. One student said that he went to school to learn to sit still in class so that he could sit still in college. Another replied, "So I can get a job." A third gave the party line, "To learn." More thoughtful kids were closer to the truth. They answered, "To learn to get along with others" and "to develop the proper attitude."

The basic reason for school, fundamental to all these answers, is self-discipline. A person who has mastered self-discipline will be successful in all aspects of life. Self-discipline enables us to grow intellectually, emotionally, and spiritually.

Encouraging my son to do well in school this year, I gave him speech number 109. (My children having memorized my speeches identify them by numbers, "That's speech number 109.")

Speech number 109 goes something like this: "I don't care if you fail to make the honor roll or if you don't become a starter in basketball, all I want is for you to do your best all of the time. If you don't do your best, you are cheating yourself. Do your best so that you can become all you can possibly be." My son unmaliciously asked, "Dad, do you always do your best?"

I paused and then had to confess, "No. I don't always do my best." I thanked my son for asking that question. That is what families are for—to encourage each other to love and to do good works. I knew I would remember the question, "Dad, do you always do your best?"

I have been struggling recently to finish writing a manuscript but have been able to find many excuses for not completing the work: I'm too tired, I'm too busy, I have other interests, etc. The morning after speech number 109, the alarm went off at 5:00 a.m. I was tempted to do what I have done many times before—turn the alarm off, roll over and go back to sleep, but, instead, I remembered my son's question, "Dad, do you always do your best?" I got out of bed and started working. Good schools ask the same question of their students, "Do you always do your best?"

Last week as I jogged on a local high school track, the temperature must have been near 100 degrees. Not a breeze stirred. The cloudless sky offered no help from the unremitting sun. Amidst this heat, on an adjacent field the football team practiced in full uniform. I could hear the pops of contact and the groans of physical effort. In the distance, the high school tennis team went through their repetitive drills.

On the edge of the football field the cheerleaders practiced their yells. The parking lot gave evidence that the band had been going through its routine and would soon return to repeat more drills. As I pounded around the track trying to cheat time and age, I contemplated the effort the students were expending. They were doing their best and I was proud of them.

Recently I have been listening to an audiocassette tape by Jerry Kramer on the legendary Green Bay Packer football coach, Vince Lombardi. Lombardi demanded excellence. He said that when you gave only 25% of your effort, you were not just giving 25% but wasting 75% of your life.

Kramer vividly remembers an especially long day on the practice field when he could do nothing right in Lombardi's eyes. Lombardi chewed on Kramer for an hour as they practiced a goal line stand. After practice, Kramer sat dejectedly in the locker room with his elbow on his knee and his chin resting on his hand, staring at the floor contemplating whether he wanted to continue with pro football. As Lombardi walked by, he paused, placed his hand on Kramer's shoulder and said, "One of these days you are going to be the best offensive guard in the NFL." Kramer said he suddenly felt a mile high, and from that day on, he began working to become the best guard in the NFL. When he determined to become the best offensive guard, he also determined to become the best husband, the best father, the best businessman he could be.

Kramer said that the most important words

Lombardi ever said to him were these, "You can if you will." Few of us are fortunate enough to have been coached by Vince Lombardi, but we can encourage each other to be the best and insist on schools that set standards of excellence. Good schools can offer this challenge to our children—"You can if you will."

The Great Teachers

⌘

Teaching, the most honorable and challenging of all professions, offers the opportunity to inspire students to become all they can possibly be. In becoming an excellent teacher one needs to remember five historical figures: Jesus Christ, Socrates, Sir William Osler, Vince Lombardi, and Will Rogers.

Jesus loved children. He said, "Let the children come to me and do not hinder them; for to such belongs the kingdom of heaven" (Matthew 19:14). If a teacher does not love children, that teacher will be ineffective and would do better to seek other employment. Jesus was also the example teacher because He taught in parables and stories. People remember better when they are taught with stories and examples. Jesus also modeled good behavior as every effective teacher does.

Socrates deserves to be remembered because he taught by asking questions. Entering into a dialogue with a student stimulates creative thought and maintains interest.

Sir William Osler, the physician's teacher, believed in work. He said, "The master word is *work*, it will make the dull man bright, the bright man brilliant, and the brilliant man steady." Osler was the model of a successful teacher. It was said of him that, "He was a modest, kind, gentleman—most informal in his daily contacts; beloved by all who looked forward to his daily visits that offered encouragement, optimism, and hope to all that he met."

Vince Lombardi, the legendary Green Bay Packer coach, always expected, and got, the best from every one of his players. Lombardi had the ability to motivate people to do better than they dreamed possible.

The life of Will Rogers reminds us that a sense of humor is vitally important in becoming an effective teacher. Rogers said, "Friends, I don't give advice. But, if I did, I'd just say that we're only on this earth for a short time, so for heaven's sake, have a few laughs and don't take things so seriously, especially yourselves. Just live your life so you wouldn't be ashamed to sell the family parrot to the town gossip." Teachers need to laugh and cultivate a sense of humor.

With these five people as models the teacher then needs to remember that students must learn the value of goals, what to do to achieve those goals, and the rewards that one gains from achieving them. The rewards for hard work can be summed up in this passage from II Corinthians 9:6, "He who sows sparingly will also reap sparingly, and he who sows bountifully will also reap bountifully." You get back in life what you send out. Hard work will be rewarded with a plentiful harvest.

All great teachers realize that helping the student learn the value of a virtuous life is more important than teaching facts. Whether teachers instruct in math, shop, English, or history, they should remember what all of us want for our children.

We want our children to have a life of wellness, prosperity, and joy. We wish for them loving friends, peace of mind, and security. We want them to learn to celebrate life. We want our children to acquire strength of character and a sense of purpose. They must learn to cultivate honesty—the ability always to tell the truth to themselves and others, integrity—the ability to keep their promises to themselves and others, faith—the belief that goodness will prevail, loyalty—being true to one's school, family, country, and team, and love—unconditional, positive regard for one's self and others.

Conveying the joy of learning is a precious privilege. The great teachers knew that and they have shown us the way.

Coaching, And Learning

✳

This week a friend and I attended a local high school basketball game. The home team coach had designed offensive and defensive plays to take advantage of the players' speed and quickness. Seeing the eager team play with precision and confidence early in the season caused us to reflect on the importance of teaching and coaching. As we watched the home team build an impressive lead, our philosophical musings kept pace with the mounting score.

We agreed that all great coaches are tremendous teachers and teaching is the noblest profession. A successful businessman, my friend told me that he had recently received the highest of all compliments. He was told that people enjoyed being around him because he was always teaching. I agreed. His attractive personality comes from his ability to convey information in an interesting and inspiring way.

We remembered that all outstanding individuals are great teachers. Business executives must teach their employees how to get the most out of their work effort. Construction bosses must teach building techniques to their laborers. Sales people teach their customers the advantage of their company's product. Psychotherapists teach their patients new ways of thinking and better methods of behavior. Good parents teach their children that life can be exciting, adventurous, and fulfilling.

We determined that all great teachers teach fundamentals. We talked of coaches who stressed the basics: Bear Bryant, Bobby Knight, Dean Smith, and Vince Lombardi.

The story goes that once after a humiliating defeat Lombardi lectured his Green Bay Packer team on the importance of fundamentals. Lombardi raged that he was a lousy teacher, the players were lousy students and that they were going to start over from basics. Lombardi reached down, picked up a football and said, "Now this is a football." Max McGee, the All Pro wide receiver, who had the reputation for being the only player who could get away with talking back to Lombardi retorted, "Hold on, coach, you're going too fast."

We also decided that all great coaches, similar to outstanding teachers, teach much more than fundamentals. They teach values that can be applied to all aspects of life. According to Jerry Kramer, named the outstanding guard in the first fifty years of the National Football League, Lombardi's instruction enabled his players to become outstanding business successes after they retired from professional football. Coach Lombardi told his players that although perfection is unattainable, they could catch excellence by chasing perfection.

Lombardi's lessons on commitment, integrity, and

the work ethic are best summarized by the statement, "You don't do things right once in a while. You do them right all of the time." The vast majority of us don't do things right all of the time. Jerry Kramer, in *Distant Replay*, says that 80 or 85% of us are taking short-cuts, looking for the easy way, either stealing from others or cheating ourselves.

One of Lombardi's most memorable thoughts has been quoted often. "All the rings, all the color, all the money, and all the display linger in the memory only a short time and are soon forgotten. But the will to win, the will to excel, these are the things that endure and are so much more important than any of the events that occasion them."

As we watched the players enjoy their ability to excel we reflected that there are many Lombardis in this world—people who stress the importance of hard work and enduring human values. In these troubled times it's easy to forget that there still remains more good than bad. If you don't believe it, come watch the coaches and the players. Be thankful for the teachers and the learners.

What Friends Teach

⌘

My friend, an expert in communication skills, taught me a valuable lesson this weekend. We had planned a leisurely night out at an elegant restaurant, but when we arrived we were informed there would be an hour wait for a table. I stormed out, grabbing my wife by the arm, with the retort, "Nothing's worth waiting an hour for."

"Wait a minute," my friend said. "You're always writing about smelling the roses. So, sit down and smell them." Under my friend's direction we moseyed (actually he moseyed, I rushed) across the street to a specialty shop and purchased the literal loaf of bread, cheese and bottle of wine. As we sat peacefully enjoying our appetizers on a bench outside the restaurant, my friend gave a lecture on personality styles, with the admonishment, "Know thyself."

He said that researchers in interpersonal relationships made popular by Wilson Learning Corporation have recognized four basic social or behavioral styles: driver, expressive, amiable, and analytical. He told me I was a driver, because I move rapidly, speak quickly and intensely, sit upright and lean forward when talking, emphatically express opinions, take risks and make decisions quickly.

"Your desk is always clean," he said. "You even alphabetize your junk mail. The few plants in your office are artificial so you won't waste time watering them. The picture of your family is at the far end of your credenza. That way you won't be distracted by looking at their photo. When you leave the office you have your car keys in your hand before you get out the front door. Your coat of arms is a stopwatch."

My friend gestured, pointed, waved his hands in the air, laughed and smiled frequently, and peppered his lecture with jokes and anecdotes. He invited passersby to share our cheese and bread; he told them the wait for a table was a long one, but worth it.

At work his desk is a mess. His file system is instant clutter. Photographs and mementos are plastered all over the office walls. His credenza looks like a greenhouse. He likes people more than projects and makes decisions more on "gut feelings" than facts. He dresses informally and when he does wear a tie, it's usually a red one. He shakes hands vigorously, smiles broadly, and laughs frequently. He emotes. He is the expressive type.

"Amiables," my friend said," are the good old boy types." You see them hosting fishing shows on television. They will make a long, slow cast into the water and say something like, "I'd rather be here than in the best hospital bed in Charlotte."

Amiables move slowly and deliberately, speak softly and express their opinions tentatively. They don't like risks and require a decade to make a decision. They chew Skoal a lot. More sophisticated ones smoke pipes.

Their desks are crowded with knickknacks and family photos. They're even messier than the expressives and wear blue jeans and boots to the office whenever possible. If they must wear a tie, they prefer a brown one. These people are reliable, dependable, steady, loyal, honest, and often very, very successful. Time, for them, is like a fine wine, to be savored and enjoyed.

The analytic types are more serious and reserved. They wear conservative suits, white shirts, and prefer broad striped blue and grey ties. They focus on facts and control their feelings. They like tasks more than people and don't particularly enjoy small talk, anecdotes and jokes.

Their desks are filled with tidy accounting ledgers. They have one plaque on the wall—from the Rotary Club. They do everything by the book. "Indeed," my friend said, "they probably wrote the book." Masters of detail, these people keep our businesses efficient.

Just as my friend finished his lecture the hostess came to tell us our table was ready. While he ate heartily and continued to thoroughly enjoy himself, I bolted my food and sat impatiently, eager to rush home and transcribe these thoughts. After all, the three hours I had set aside for "fun" were about over.

Benjamin Franklin's Virtues

�֍

Anyone desiring to be a better person would do well to read Benjamin Franklin's *Autobiography*. Franklin, in his masterful style writes, "... I conceived the bold and arduous project of arriving at moral perfection. I wished to live without committing any fault at any time; I would conquer all that either natural inclination, custom, or company might lead me into."

Franklin made a notebook listing 13 virtues he wished to achieve. He ruled the page in seven columns, one for each day of the week. At the end of each day he checked every fault that he had committed on each virtue. Here are Franklin's 13 virtues and his comments on each:

1. Temperance—eat not to dullness; drink not to elevation.
2. Silence—speak not but what may benefit others or yourself; avoid trifling conversation.
3. Order—let all your things have their places; let each part of your business have its time.
4. Resolution—resolve to perform what you ought; perform without fail what you resolve.
5. Frugality—make no expense but to do good to others or yourself; *i.e.*, waste nothing.

6. Industry—lose no time; be always employed in something useful; cut off all unnecessary actions.

7. Sincerity—use no hurtful deceit; think innocently and justly, and, if you speak, speak accordingly.

8. Justice—wrong none by doing injuries or omitting the benefits that are your duty.

9. Moderation—avoid extremes; forbear resenting injuries so much as you think they deserve.

10. Cleanliness—tolerate no uncleanliness in body, clothes, or habitation.

11. Tranquility—be not disturbed by trifles, or at accidents common or unavoidable.

12. Chastity—rarely use venery but for health or offspring, never to dullness, weakness, or injury to your own or another's peace or reputation. (Franklin was not a one-woman man).

13. Humility—imitate Jesus or Socrates.

Although your virtues may differ from Franklin's, you may find helpful his technique of writing them down and regularly checking yourself on your progress. Most of us spend our time just getting through the day. We rarely reflect on what we have done each day, and another week vanishes followed quickly by the months and years. We have marked time, but achieved nothing.

All of us could be better than we are. There is always room for improvement. To lead a virtuous life requires contemplation on virtue. We must think, as Franklin did, about what is important to us and we must persist in striving for a higher life.

As Franklin writes, "Tho I never arrived at the perfection I had been so ambitious of obtaining, but fell far short of it, yet I was by the endeavour, a better and a happier man than I otherwise should have been if I had not attempted it."

The Common Sense Philosophers

�֍

Depression—that blue, down-in-the-dumps feeling—is ubiquitous. Over the course of a lifetime one out of four people will have a major depression characterized by the inability to function normally at work and home. All of us, however, have milder forms of depression from time to time. No matter how much you have and how personable you are, there is a tendency to become depressed. As song writer, performer and common sense philosopher, Dolly Parton, said:

"I get into moods. Depression is part of life. It's a natural emotion. If you never get depressed, you're never getting down deep enough to think about things. Nobody is up all the time unless they're liars, phonies, hypocrites, or unless something in their brains ain't working. But I won't allow myself to be depressed more than just three days in a row. When it happens, I say, 'Now, look here, you just sit down with a piece of paper and write down all the good things you have to be grateful for. Then get up and get (going). Fix yourself up. Talk to someone . . . Be grateful your man loves you.'"

Mary Kay Ash, C.E.O. of Mary Kay Cosmetics and another practical philosopher, reiterates Dolly Parton's statements. Mary Kay says there are three things that make life worth living: l) someone to love and who loves you in return; 2) work that you enjoy; and 3) something to look forward to. Message: activity and love cure misery.

Dr. De la Pena, a research associate in psycho-physiology at the University of Texas Medical School, reports that the mind-body system requires new challenges to stay in balance. If your life has lost its zest, if your daily routine has become tedious, if your motto is "ho-hum", you may be on the verge of depression. The boredom produced by too little stimulation is as great, or greater, stress than that generated by too much stimulation.

If you're bored then you may find your mind turns to depression anger, fear, or worry. Instead of filling your mind with negative emotions, try writing down your worries, crumpling the paper and throwing it in the trash. That will help put your concerns in proper perspective.

Because worry is negative goal setting, practice emptying your mind daily of negative thoughts and replacing them with peaceful, tranquil thoughts. Instead of participating in fretful conversations, inject faith in your statements by saying something like, "Nothing is hopeless for those who have plans." Surround yourself with people who talk positively and are action oriented.

While activity prevents boredom we must also take time to enjoy life—we must cultivate balance between overwork and underwork. After basketball coach Bill

Foster, who guided Duke against Kentucky for the national championship in 1978, suffered quadruple bypass surgery, he looked back on his glory days at Duke and said, "Those were my most memorable days in coaching . . . but I never did enjoy it. I don't know what it was. It didn't really sink in and that's my own fault . . . I just never relaxed."

Prior to his stress-related heart attack Foster said that he thought of himself as Superman. "I loved to work twenty hours and sleep four." Since his heart attack Foster has become more relaxed and peaceful. He says, "I'm finding that I enjoy my family more and they enjoy me more. Before, I was going around with my head in the wrong places. I was worried about the next game, worried about this guy not playing, worried about what some guy had said in an article in the newspaper, things that were totally out of my control."

Lee Iacocca, Chief Executive Officer and President of Chrysler Corporation, says, "Since college I've worked hard during the week and, except for crises, kept my weekends free for family and recreation. Every Sunday night I get the adrenaline going again by making a list of what I want to accomplish during the coming week. I'm amazed at the number of people who can't seem to control their own schedules. 'Boy,' some say, 'I worked so hard last year I didn't even take a vacation.' I say, 'You dummy. You mean to tell me you can take the responsibility of an eighty-million dollar project and you can't take two weeks out of the year to have some fun?'"

A time for rest and relaxation enables the mind and body to regenerate and renew themselves. Rest is an excellent use of time and properly scheduled recreation will increase rather than decrease productivity.

To fight depression, then, requires activity properly balanced with recreation and rest. A life of love, activity and balance cures misery.

Why Aristotle?

✳

We study philosophy to better understand those things we already know. To clearly understand ourselves and our lives there is no better philosopher to begin with than Aristotle, Plato's student. Aristotle had what modern philosopher Mortimer J. Adler calls "uncommon" common sense.

Aristotle tells us that to live as well as possible we must develop a plan for living. He expands on the wisdom of Socrates. Socrates teaches that the unexamined life is not worth living. Aristotle declares that the unplanned life is not worth examining. He uses logic to prove that happiness is the ultimate end, that it defines the good life that everyone seeks. There are many unproductive plans for living—plans that will not lead us toward Aristotle's ultimate end—the good life. Happiness doesn't just occur. Aristotle tells us it is the product of a process. We can plan for happiness.

Developing a plan for living well allows us to acquire all the things we need and guides us to a complete realization of our capabilities. Not all the things we want, but do not need, turn out to be good for us. Some things that are not harmful to us may still interfere with our getting that which is best for us.

Among those things that are best for us are health and enough wealth to obtain food, drink, shelter and clothing. A certain amount of wealth allows us to live well, but too much wealth can prevent us from getting what Aristotle calls goods of the soul. Those things good for the soul are knowledge, love, friendship, self-esteem and honor.

Wealth is desirable only as a means of living well. Wealth is not desirable for its own sake. Wealth and bodily pleasures are limited goods. We can want more wealth and bodily pleasures than we need and more than we need is not good for us. Knowledge, skill, and the pleasures of the soul are goods of which we cannot have too much; they are unlimited goods. More of them is always better.

Aristotle's prescription for the good life directs us to develop a good moral character. A good moral character enables us to acquire bodily goods (health), external goods (wealth), and goods of the soul (psychological goods). To develop good moral character requires good habits of choice. The name that Aristotle gives to good habits is translated as "virtue." A good life can be lived by making morally virtuous choices and decisions that are good for the soul.

Regrets indicate that we have made the wrong choices. Choices that leave us with no regrets contribute to our pursuit of happiness. Moral virtue, the habit of making right choices, enables us to put correct goods in the right order, limits bodily goods and wealth when they should be limited, and allows us to put aside things we want when they interfere with obtaining things of lasting value. The virtuous person regularly makes the right choices and time and time again these correct choices lead to happiness and good memories.

Temperance, the act of habitually resisting the temptation to over-indulge, enables us to resist short term pleasures for the sake of long term benefits. With temperance we seek wealth as a means to other goods, and not as an end in itself.

Courage is the habit of taking pains to do what we ought to do for the sake of a good life. It takes courage to get knowledge and other skills that we ought to have, because acquiring knowledge and skill may be painful and hard to do. Trying to live well is not easy, but the satisfaction that comes from a life well lived is worth all the effort it takes.

Generosity of love, not the obligations of justice, impels one individual to help another obtain those things needed for the good life. Others have a right to expect that we keep the promises we make, that we tell the truth, that we pay our debts, that we do not steal, that we do not injure their health, or kill them, that we do not interfere with their freedom, that we do not make false statements that would injure their reputation, and that we do nothing that might impede their pursuit of happiness. Justice can help individuals in their pursuit of happiness, but love can inspire us all to live well.

Aristotle proves what we innately know—that the

virtuous life is the life best lived. Reading Aristotle and re-framing Aristotle's thought stimulates us to reason and reconsider and impels us to lead the life that he encour-ages. Aristotle makes sense, uncommonly good sense.

Universities And The Freedom To Learn

This past weekend my family, in preparation for my daughter entering college next year, visited three fine universities in our state. As we toured the beautiful campuses, we were reminded that a university is more than bricks and mortar. What makes a great university are the professors and students and the cultivation of an intellectual climate that demands excellence in learning to think.

The importance of the next four years in my daughter's life cannot be overestimated. The university she chooses will shape the career she will pursue, the life she will live and the kind of human being she will become. These four years mark civilization's only chance to win her.

If my daughter is to have hope of a higher life, she must learn to think. The prejudices of religion, class and family must be challenged and reshaped. To reason clearly she must study history, philosophy, literature, religion, anthropology and art. Only after broad and deep study will she be able to abandon authority in favor of human reason. She must become more than a tourist in the liberal arts if she is to develop the freedom to become all she can possibly be.

In *The Republic* Plato introduces the famous myth of the cave proposed by Socrates in which men are like prisoners in a cave facing away from the light. Unable to see themselves or anyone else because they are shackled, the men observe only the shadows of things on the wall in front of them, not realizing that the reality is something quite different from the shadows. The student is like a man who leaves the cave, comes to know things as they really are, and returns to help the shackled men who think that shadows make up the true world. A great university, then, represents the world of ideas where students learn to distinguish truth from shadows.

To be released from the shackles of ignorance one must be exposed to a wide range of experience and thought. Allan Bloom in *The Closing of the American Mind* says "A serious life means being fully aware of the alternatives, thinking about them with all the intensity one brings to bear on life and death questions, in full recognition that every choice is a great risk with necessary consequences that are hard to bear."

A great university provides students with experiences they can have nowhere else. It teaches self-examination, articulates nobility, instructs in virtue and encourages the pursuit of peace.

How does one determine if a university is a great one—that it stands for truth, learning and the higher virtues? Here are some questions to ask:

* Are the students bright, inquisitive, and eager to learn?

* Do the students come from a wide variety of experiences and geographical locations?
* Are the classes taught by full professors?
* Does the university have a strong liberal arts requirement? Is the student expected to learn how to write and to understand literature, religion, philosophy, history and politics?
* Does the university have a strong fine arts department—will the student be exposed to music, art and drama?
* Does the campus ambiance and beauty encourage study?
* Does the university have an outstanding library?
* Does the social structure teach more than beer drinking, belching and bedding? Does it teach refinement?
* Does the administration demand ethical behavior in their athletic and development programs?
* Is the student required to live on campus at least two years?
* Is there a unifying school spirit on campus?
* Do the university's alumni have positions of outstanding leadership and success?
* Do the alumni support the university?

During these next four years, I want my daughter's ideas refined and her personality polished. I want for her both culture and common sense. I want her beliefs challenged and for her to re-think all issues to learn what is good, what is wise and what is just.

I want her to understand that dogma limits the

perception of God's goodness. Through free study I want her to learn that the soul is immortal and the just and the wise prosper in this life and in the hereafter. I want her to discover that God is a kind, good and giving God and that the virtuous life is the life best lived. A great university will enable her to make these discoveries.

Knight Lessons

In 1987 my son and I had the privilege of attending the NCAA Final Four Basketball Tournament. The highlight of the weekend was Sunday's press conference where Indiana's Bobby Knight elegantly espoused his philosophy of achievement.

Knight, who the following evening would win his third championship, has received mixed media coverage. While almost everyone agrees that he understands the intricacies of basketball, some question his methods. Knight is either loved or hated. The press conference explained why. Knight seems to have two controversial character traits. He uses profane language that is more salty than a seasoned seaman, and he has uncontrolled temper outbursts that would rival a hungry baby with a wet diaper.

But Knight does have a magnetic personality. The force of his personality comes from his intellect and his firm stand on issues. He has the courage of his convictions and is unswayed by others' opinions. He does not base his self-worth on what others think.

Force of personality is a term often used, but seldom explained. Most of us have average skills, average intellect, average looks, and average personalities.

Bobby Knight is not average. The man's pursuit of excellence, his courage, his intelligence, and his inner arrogance make for an extraordinary personality.

Knight's powerful personality is shaped by his single-minded pursuit of excellence. Since Peters and Waterman's book, *In Search of Excellence,* "the pursuit of excellence" has become an overused phrase. Excellence is the master word of the '80's. Though the term may suffer from overexposure, I can think of no better way to describe Knight than as a master example of a pursuer of excellence. Knight said that he wanted to be remembered as, "a guy who got the most out of what he had." That's what the pursuit of excellence is about—getting the most out of what we have been given.

To get the most out of our talents requires single-mindedness. No one gets the most out of what he has without discipline. Discipline is the difference between mediocrity and greatness. With discipline the average becomes outstanding. Perhaps that's why Knight admires his senior guard, Steve Alford. Alford is not big, strong, or quick, but, through discipline and practice, he became the second leading scorer in Big Ten basketball history.

If Knight is the guru of basketball excellence, Alford is the example. All young basketball players who dream of becoming an All-American and playing in the Final Four would do well to emulate Alford. Alford is average in every way except one—self-discipline. He had the self-discipline to practice and constantly improve his shooting ability. He had the self-discipline to work on his defense and his ability to get the open shot. Alford is "a guy who got the most out of what he had."

The power of Knight's personality is probably summarized by a statement that he made at the press conference. He said, "I'm the only guy who has to answer to me." Knight doesn't care what others think about him, but he is a perfectionist who puts pressure on himself to achieve all that he can become. He also puts pressure on his basketball players to do their absolute best.

Knight is his own man. There are no grey zones in his life. Everything is either black or white. The ability to stand firm against all criticism is probably the most important factor in Knight's magnetic personality. His courage is what attracts some people to him and repels others. Most people progress through life wishy-washy and lukewarm. Many of us are, as Shakespeare says, "...a feather for every wind that blows." Knight's single-minded drive to perfection is so strong that his personality would resist hurricane force winds.

Knight has keen powers of observation. He has studied the greats in sports history. He liked to watch Johnny Bench, whom he views as the best catcher who ever lived, warm up the pitcher between innings. Knight noticed that Bench was so good at his job that he could talk to the umpire, the fans in the crowd, or the next batter while moving his glove around as he caught the baseball. Thousands of people have seen Johnny Bench play baseball, but probably very few have watched him warm up the pitchers. Real students notice the little extras that go unnoticed by the common man. Attention to detail marks great people.

All great athletes, outstanding business people, and successful volunteers have an inner arrogance that helps propel them to greatness. They believe they can get the job done. When the game is on the line, these All-Stars want to be the batter, the free throw shooter, and the coach. They believe in themselves. Inner arrogance differs from empty boasting or cockiness. People with inner arrogance allow their actions to speak for them.

Bobby Knight may inspire either devotion or criticism, but, to a close observer, he exemplifies the pursuit of excellence, courage, intelligence and "inner arrogance." We could all learn from him.

It's Great To Be Alive

⌘

The NCAA Final Four Basketball Tournament, one of the nation's premiere sporting events, allows the four top basketball teams to gather for a shoot-out to determine the nation's top basketball team. The media hype and the sixty-four team tournament that leads to the championship event have fans piqued to a frenzy. The crowds are always loud, boisterous and happy; the teams, intensely competitive; and the games fast-paced and exciting.

Having been fortunate to have attended the last three tournaments, I have found the highlight of the weekend to be the Sunday press conference in which the starting line-ups and coaches for both teams give an extended three-hour press conference. This year's tournament, pitting two Big Eight teams, Kansas and Oklahoma, against each other, was marked by the diametrically opposed personalities of the two coaches—studious Larry Brown versus "good ole' boy" Billy Tubbs.

Kansas head coach Larry Brown was measured and thoughtful in his approach to the press conference questions. Brown was self-revealing, however, when he told the press that he had such an obsessive drive toward perfection that he never allowed himself any freedom to experience the joy of daily activities. He remembered being told by one of his assistant coaches several years ago, "Slow down and smell the roses." Brown said that he didn't even know what his friend meant.

Brown said his turnaround began when one of his star players, Archie Marshall, suffered a career-ending knee injury in a crucial game at Madison Square Garden. Marshall, who was a star player in the Final Four appearance of Kansas in 1986, had seriously injured his knee in the semi-final game against Duke that year. He had worked diligently to rehabilitate his knee, and he was counted on to invigorate the team's march to the championship. When Marshall injured his other knee at the Garden it was apparent that he would never play basketball again. Brown rushed out onto the court and, under the eyes of 14,000 fans and a national television audience, cried bitter tears for his heroic player.

Later, when the team lost a crucial game to Kansas, Brown said he decided that he needed to attempt to enjoy life more. Brown said, "No matter what happens I have never really enjoyed much. I never allowed myself to enjoy experiences at the moment. But, since the middle of January when we lost to Kansas State, it's been the first time in my life where I really enjoyed what was going on." Brown's serious mood at the press conference, however, clearly showed that the day before the championship game wasn't a time for fun.

In contrast, Oklahoma coach Billy Tubbs was a fun-loving, "sock it to 'em" coach whose repartee with the press had everybody enjoying his openness and enthusiasm. Tubbs, who has been criticized for running up the score, told the press, "We're going to get every point we can get. That's the way I played and that's the way it is and it's not going to change." Tubbs went on to say, "Our whole philosophy is when we hit the floor for practice or a game, no one is going to have more intensity or work harder than we do." Tubbs also has confidence. "When we looked at our schedule before the season, we didn't see a game on there that would take a miracle to win. It's a rare occasion when we step on the floor and don't think we can win."

It was apparent that most of the 750 media crew who attended Sunday's press conference were on Larry Brown's side. Billy was simply having too much fun for the press to take his coaching seriously. Despite Kansas' rags to riches story—they had overcome adversity the whole year, losing three starters to injuries and academic problems, overcoming devastating losses and barely getting a bid to the tournament, Billy Tubbs' flamboyant personality won me over.

We need more people in this world who enjoy life to the fullest. Billy said that every day he reports to his staff with the emphatic statement, "It's great to be alive." Rather than guarding his words and thoughtfully answering every question, Tubbs simply enjoyed himself and savored every moment in the spotlight.

Listening to Larry and laughing with Billy reminded me that whoever wins or loses, whatever defeats or successes we have, "It's great to be alive." ⌘

Being True To Yourself With Passion

⌘

For the past three months I have been sitting in my study each night, hand on the telephone, waiting for a call inviting me to give the commencement address for my daughter's high school graduation. I thought I was a shoo-in for the job. After all, anyone who would readily accept the job as Cleanup Chairman for the all-night graduation dance deserves some sort of honor. Unfortunately, no one called. I wrote the speech anyway. Here it is.

On commencement occasions the speaker feels the duty to give words of wisdom, advice and inspiration. Words of wisdom from me would seem out of place, since I just accepted the job as Cleanup Chairman. As for advice, I would suggest to you graduates that it's okay to feel uncertain. Adulthood might have come upon you before you're certain you're ready for it. Most of the time I think I'm not ready for my adulthood either. And if you get into trouble, remember what Robert Frost said, "Home is the place where, when you have to go there, they have to take you in."

Now for the inspiration—a much more sobering task. Most important: have integrity. Integrity means keeping your promises to yourself and honoring your commitments to others. Always tell the truth. Truth telling compensates for a poor memory. When you tell the truth you don't have to remember what you said. But more important, because so few people tell the truth, your integrity will distinguish you as an honorable person.

Being true to yourself means doing the best you can with shooting baskets in the gym all alone; it means staying in the music lab past midnight practicing the cello; it means spending week-ends in the library. These sacrifices are the only way you can be the best you can be.

Being true to yourself means ridding yourself of caution and timidity caused by an acute fear of failure. Fear of failure is much more incapacitating than failure. Nothing great was ever accomplished without numerous false starts and setbacks. Fear of failure is the great destroyer—it keeps you from trying anything.

Being true to yourself means you don't listen to those who say you can't. You ignore people who say you're taking too big a risk. You don't listen to that little inner voice that says, "They're smarter than you; they're more talented; they're luckier."

Being true to yourself means having the guts to take chances. Be bold. Don't let trouble defeat you. Walk closely with God so that nothing can disturb your peace of mind.

The force that disciplines and motivates all great achievers and without which life is flat and unprofitable is the single word—passion. Nothing in life that is worthwhile was ever achieved without a burning passion to achieve it. Passion allows us to get excited about details and it's the intense involvement in details that determines the quality of anything in life.

If you passionately follow a path that interests you and bring to the trip a sense of self-worth and cooperation obsessed by the conviction that you can move others by your efforts, then you will be worthy of your own respect. Passionate people do not make success or failure the criteria by which they live. Passion is the joy of getting there. Success is a trap that can prevent you from continuing to enjoy working toward the achievement of a goal. Whether you make a lot of money or not you'll have a wonderful time if you are passionate about what you're doing.

Remember it's up to you to create your own meaning in this absurd world. It's up to you to enjoy yourself in a life of your own choosing. Be certain to laugh each day. People who are laughing generally don't hurt each other. Don't take yourself too seriously, but don't lose your ambition. Laugh at yourself, but don't doubt yourself. Let your wit shield you against bias and criticism.

Delight in the unique person that you are and others will be drawn to you. A flash of enthusiasm, the excitement of anticipation, a spark of anger, a hearty laugh—all these emotions make you more real to others—and more intriguing. Do everything with great intensity and flair. Above all, enjoy life.

The life you lead is up to you. How you respond to trouble is your decision. The impact you make on others is your choice. Choose truth, choose passion, choose joy and God will always be with you to guide you, help you and comfort you.   ❁

For Wisdom Never Dies

When I heard of my grandfather's death, an overwhelming emptiness flooded my soul. How could I go on? What would life be without him? I missed him so. He was a part of me. A part of me died with him.

The memories came rushing back. I was eight years old, sitting on the pier, fishing. He showed me how to bait the hook with the grasshoppers we had caught and placed in a jar. He demonstrated how to tug the line when the fish struck. He caught eleven perch; I caught five. It was strange that I would remember the number. I can still vividly see the fish on the stringer. We had a grand time laughing and talking like men.

Then there was the memory of riding across the pasture. I was on Steeldust; he was on Ribbon. He rode smoothly, beautifully erect. I bounced so violently that I thought I would fall. When we crested the hill we looked out over the pasture as it sloped to the wooded creek and in the far distance he pointed out our home. It seemed a vast land that my grandfather owned and he appeared larger than life. How could he die? Not my grandfather.

Then there was a time much later when I was newly married and brought my wife for a visit. We played forty-two. He showed her how to get a good hand by spinning the chair three times before sitting down. She fell instantly in love with him. He had a way of doing that—his gentle kindness and good humor made his virility even more powerful. He was a man's man and a woman's man and now he was dead. How could that happen?

I remember him sitting in the living room reading. He was always reading and learning. He was always giving to others and encouraging them to do good for mankind. How could he die?

I tried not to remember his deteriorating condition in later years. The leukemia sapped his physical strength but not his spiritual power. Although the rest of his body wasted away, to the end his hands remained powerfully strong. He always had such strong hands, symbolic of a strong soul perhaps. And now he was dead and I felt empty, spiritually and physically drained.

As a psychiatrist I knew the stages of grief that we all pass through: denial, anger, rationalization, depression, and finally acceptance. During the first few weeks you are numb. Everything you do takes extra effort, like walking in wet sand. Next, you begin to feel a violent anger welling up. You blame the doctors, or God, or yourself. You're mad at everyone and everything. This anger passes and you begin to second-guess yourself and others. You try to make sense of the death. You search for alternatives. Then you become profoundly depressed. You cry a lot. You feel empty. Life, for you, has no meaning.

Many times these stages are all wrapped into one and the feelings may descend on you simultaneously, or different feelings may come at different times of the day. Eventually, through experiencing and talking about your feelings with others, through tears and grieving, acceptance comes.

Although I understood the process in detail, at the moment of my own grieving these stages were merely intellectual postulations. I didn't see how I could get through it or get over it, but in time I did. Time heals all wounds and mends all scars. "Shovel them under and let me work—I am the grass; I cover all."

I am stronger now than when my grandfather was alive. I have taken in his character traits and see myself as an extension of his spirit. I know his spirit is watching over me and comforting me and wanting to help me. He continues to live this earthly life through me and I become more spiritual through his comfort and concern.

As I write this, tears come. But they are tears of joy. Because my grandfather lived and I knew him and loved him I am a better man, a far, far better man than I would otherwise have been. His presence is still powerfully with me every day and I think of him with joy and laughter and peace and strength. Because of him I will do good and I will continue to strive to help others and the world will be a better place. Grief, resolved, gives us the power to be kind and assures us that life goes on forever and ever.

ORDER FORM

LIFEWORKS PUBLISHING
7967 TURF PARADISE LANE
FAIR OAKS RANCH, TEXAS 78015
(210) 698-2758 / FAX: (210) 698-9158

QTY.	ITEM	UNIT	EXTENSION
	LEVERAGE YOUR TIME: BALANCE YOUR LIFE	Soft Cover: $15.00	
	A LIFE WELL LIVED	Soft Cover: $15.00	
	50 WAYS TO KEEP YOUR LOVER	Soft Cover: $10.00	
	JIM REID'S WINNING BASKETBALL	Soft Cover: $10.00	
	THE PEOPLE'S PSYCHIATRY: EVERYTHING YOU WANTED TO KNOW ABOUT YOURSELF (AND OTHERS) BUT WERE AFRAID TO ASK	Soft Cover: $19.95	
	GOD DRIVES A PICKUP TRUCK By Buckner Fanning	Soft Cover: $16.95	
	TOTAL SELF-HELP: THE FUNDAMENTAL PRINCIPALS OF PERSONAL GROWTH	Tape Series: $50.00	
	LIFE WORKS	One Year Subscription: $20.00	
		SUB-TOTAL:	
		TEXAS RESIDENTS: Add 7.75% Sales Tax:	
		Shipping & Handling: $3.50 per item	
		TOTAL ENCLOSED:	

PLEASE SHIP TO:

Name: _____

Mailing Address: _____

City, State and Zip: _____

Daytime Telephone: _____

❏ Please send information on presentations by LifeWorks speakers.

❏ Please send information on quantity discounts for the following title(s):

_____

_____

_____

_____

ABOUT THE AUTHOR

Dr. Walker is a psychiatrist, publisher and writer. He and his wife, Victoria, an international protocol consultant, have been married for 34 years. They have two happily married children and one grandchild.

Dr. Walker speaks at banquets that refuse to compensate their speakers because no one will pay to hear him speak. He has found that at these banquets some of the people listen to him some of the time. This gratifies Dr. Walker, because wherever else he goes, no one listens to him any of the time.

His wife, Victoria, elects not to attend his speeches because having heard him speak in public one time was enough for her. She does, however, take Dr. Walker with her on her protocol/etiquette presentations as an example of social inadequacy. The audience begins to relax when they realize that their social gaffes could never match Dr. Walker's.